# quick-fix
## gluten free

Also by Robert M. Landolphi

*Gluten Free Every Day Cookbook*

# quick-fix
## gluten free

### robert m. landolphi

Andrews McMeel
Publishing, LLC

Kansas City • Sydney • London

Andrews McMeel Publishing, LLC
an Andrews McMeel Universal company
1130 Walnut Street, Kansas City, Missouri 64106

www.andrewsmcmeel.com

11 12 13 14 15 RR2 10 9 8 7 6 5 4 3 2 1

ISBN: 978-1-4494-0293-8    *4765 6607  1/12*

Library of Congress Control Number: 2010937754

Cover design by Tim Lynch
Cover photography and page xiv by Thomas Gibson
Other photos courtesy iStockphoto.com

www.glutenfreechefrob.com

ATTENTION: SCHOOLS AND BUSINESSES
Andrews McMeel books are available at quantity discounts with bulk purchase for educational, business, or sales promotional use. For information, please e-mail the Andrews McMeel Publishing Special Sales Department: specialsales@amuniversal.com

This book is dedicated to my three sons,
Joseph, Andrew, and Stephen, and to
St. Lawrence (patron saint of cooks)

# contents

# acknowledgments

Wow! I can't believe it—*Quick-Fix Gluten Free* is done! I often speak of the miracles in my life, and completing this second book, amid my wife's third pregnancy and delivery and welcoming a newborn into our lives, is nothing short of miraculous. I now need to thank the many wonderful people who have graced my life and helped take this book from possibility to reality.

My gratitude begins with the numerous people who bought my first book, embraced it with enthusiasm, and then shared, in phone calls and e-mails, the joy it had brought back into their kitchens and their lives. The overwhelming response and requests for more are what motivated me to compose the recipes for *Quick-Fix Gluten Free* and kept me burning the midnight oil (and the 3:00 A.M. oil when you have a nursing baby in the house) to get the book done. Thank you to Beth Hillson, cookbook author and celiac expert, who shared her wealth of knowledge about the ever-changing gluten-free industry while providing valuable advice and being a friend. To my literary agent, Susan Ginsberg, thank you for your wise counsel and your "gentle reminders" that deadlines were approaching. I want to thank the dedicated staff at my publishing house, Andrews McMeel, for recognizing the increasing need for gluten-free resources and for giving me another opportunity to make a difference in a few lives. Gratitude is extended to Lane Butler, who edited each word with talent and tact, and to Tammie Barker, who worked tirelessly in promoting both books—here's hoping that your work pays off again! I am grateful to my friends at Udi's, who allowed me to be creative and experimental with their incredible baked goods and then went out of their way to support me in my endeavors. I also want to acknowledge the work done by my webmaster, Derrick Ellis, who constructed and continually updates an excellent website at www.glutenfreechefrob.com, as well as my friend Gail Merrill, whose creativity always leads me to new ideas.

Loving thanks to my wife, Angela, and to my young sons, who often endured eating the same meal 3 or 4 nights in a row until I got it right—who says you can't have Pretzel-Crusted Tilapia with Dijon Cream Sauce every day for a week? And to all of my friends and family members who kept extra copies of *Gluten Free Every Day Cookbook* in their homes, offices, and the trunks of their cars, shamelessly peddling it to anyone they met who said, "I just started a gluten free diet." Isn't life funny?

It is with true devotion that I acknowledge and thank the saints that have constantly interceded on my behalf during the trials that occur in day-to-day life and who inspired me to continue this project on the days that were hardest. Specifically, I thank St. Pio of Pietrelcina, St. Joseph, St. Andrew, and St. Stephen (after whom my three sons are named). And finally, thanks to the Lord and His Blessed Mother, who are always there, watching over my family and providing whatever is needed on any given occasion. You have blessed me with so much, and I thank you with all my heart.

# foreword

People with gluten and wheat sensitivities are indeed fortunate to have a resource like Robert Landolphi's *Quick-Fix Gluten Free* cookbook, a comprehensive go-to collection of family favorites that everyone can enjoy. We are fortunate in many ways. We live in a global community that is rich in gluten-free choices from products and services to recipes and medical research. And it's all for us.

But it wasn't always the case.

When I was diagnosed with celiac disease in 1976, I was alone—no cooks by my side, no support groups where I could have my questions answered, and no products to purchase. The doctor handed me a photo of my biopsy and told me I would recover completely as long as I followed a gluten-free diet. Then he turned me loose with these words, "Just avoid gluten."

I was living in Germany and attended culinary school so I could learn to eat defensively. That meant understanding how foods were made, how soups were thickened, which meats were dusted in flour, etc., so I could ask the right questions when I ate in a restaurant. I was determined that being gluten free was not going to stop me from enjoying life, enjoying food.

Being a "glass half full" person, I quickly realized that the recipes from cooking school held other secrets. If I removed flour and other offending ingredients and replaced them with the ingredients that were safe, I could create a recipe that came close to the real thing, only gluten free.

At that moment, I did not realize my future was in these recipes and techniques. But when I returned to the United States and began blending dry ingredients for breads, pancakes, and cakes, it was the beginning of something much larger, the foundation for the Gluten-Free Pantry, a gourmet baking mix company that I started in 1993.

Even then, I didn't imagine a huge market for my gourmet baking mixes. According to medical statistics at that time, only 1 in 1,000 people had celiac disease. I rarely met another celiac person. Even my local support group was tiny, with just five members.

By the time I sold Gluten-Free Pantry in 2005, celiac disease and the gluten-free diet were turning heads everywhere.

And look where we are today:

- More than 3 million people (1 in 133) have celiac disease, and only a small fraction have been diagnosed.
- Gluten-free products represent a 2.6-billion-dollar industry that will grow by 20 percent every year.
- Between 15 and 45 million people are estimated to have gluten intolerance.
- Restaurants routinely offer gluten-free menus.
- Gluten-free labeling regulations are in the pipeline, and legislation requiring manufacturers to disclose the presence of wheat in products makes it easier to shop for gluten-free foods.

These are amazing accomplishments I could not have envisioned when I was diagnosed or when I founded Gluten-Free Pantry.

Some call me a "pioneer" in the gluten-free industry, but I was simply looking for ways to survive deliciously when nothing else existed. Rob Landolphi is the "new pioneer" on the gluten-free frontier.

The gluten-free world is divided into those who arrive in this business wowed by the numbers and those who are touched by a personal need and a desire to help. Rob Landolphi falls into the second category. He knows firsthand that meals can be a challenge, especially when a special diet is involved. When his wife, Angela, was diagnosed with celiac disease, he put heart to hearth to create great meals that everyone in the family could enjoy. Now Rob brings these great foods to you and your family. As a trained chef, he sets the bar high, feeding all of us food that is as good as anything we've left behind—dishes like Pistachio-and-Mustard-Encrusted Lamb Chops, Scallop and Shrimp Asiago Risotto, and Sweet Cheese Crêpes with Caramelized Peaches and Granola.

While many of his recipes are inspired by his own family's likes, this book also contains recipes requested by readers, including Southern-Style Chicken and Dumplings, the Middle Eastern salad called Fattoush, and Thai Coconut Curried Shrimp over rice stick noodles. And there are simple treats we all miss—Corn Dogs, Fried Mozzarella Sticks with Easy Spicy Marinara, and Lazy Lady's Apple Crisp.

Today we have so many resources it's hard to know which ones to pick. Now that you've opened this book, I'd like to say, "Welcome. You're making a wise choice." You are about to embark on a delicious gluten-free journey. Cooking with Rob Landolphi and his *Quick-Fix Gluten Free* recipes will have your tummy grinning from ear to ear.

Happy gluten-free cooking,

Beth Hillson

Founder, Gluten-Free Pantry
Food Editor, Living Without
President, American Celiac Disease Alliance

# introduction

Those of you who have read my first cookbook know that the gluten-free lifestyle has been a lifesaver and a blessing for those in my family. In a nutshell, in the late nineties, my wife, Angela, became mysteriously ill, fatigued, and in pain. Her suffering was multifaceted and long lasting and seemed to have no identifiable origin. Her symptoms included random headaches, joint and muscle pain and numbness, excessive fatigue, digestive upset, weight loss, rashes, thinning hair and nails, and a complete cessation of ovulation, leading to nearly eight years of heart-wrenching infertility. Her doctors were evasive and dismissive and could not give her any set answers as to why she felt so awful and why we could not start a much desired family. They offered suggestions of multiple sclerosis, Lyme disease, Epstein-Barr virus, chronic fatigue syndrome, etc., and sent her on her way with no treatment plan. After so many incorrect diagnoses, she learned she had celiac disease. Finding the gluten-free diet was just short of miraculous, and it completely revolutionized our lives and restored Angela's health. Without it, Angela would not be the same person today, and we would not be surrounded by the love and laughter of our three beautiful, cherished young sons. Our experience with the diet and the need to find truly good, innovative gluten-free foods inspired me to start creating gluten-free recipes and to assemble them into cookbooks to help anyone who wants to embrace the gluten-free lifestyle

Celiac disease is an autoimmune disorder that currently affects 2 to 3 million Americans. In addition, there is an ever-growing population classified as nonceliac gluten intolerant. Many people wonder exactly what the difference is between celiac disease and gluten intolerance. Peter H.R. Green, M.D., gastroenterologist and researcher, explains that celiac disease is a multisystem disorder that begins in the small intestine. The disease is triggered by gluten, the primary protein found in wheat, barley, and rye grains, which causes an inflammatory response in the cells that line the small intestine and results in the flattening of the intestinal villi. It is considered an autoimmune disorder, a digestive disorder, and a genetic disorder.[1]

Dr. Stephen Wangen, a gluten-intolerant physician and cofounder of the IBS Treatment Center of Seattle, Washington, notes in his book, *Healthier Without Wheat*, that although little research has been done on the prevalence of gluten intolerance there are millions of people who do not have celiac disease but manifest symptoms that are very similar when they ingest wheat and gluten proteins.[2] He believes that probably 10 percent of the population is nonceliac gluten intolerant, which would mean that somewhere in the neighborhood of 30 million Americans suffer from it. Even more recent research indicates that the true numbers exceed or double those figures.

One of the major differences between the two is that celiac disease can be assessed and diagnosed by a physician or gastroenterologist through a biopsy of the small intestine, antibody blood tests, or saliva or blood DNA tests. Gluten intolerance, however, has no lab tests to diagnose it. It is identified by removing wheat and gluten from the diet and noticing changes in how you feel, the restoration of your health, or the cessation of your symptoms.

When I began writing my first cookbook, *Gluten Free Every Day Cookbook*, Angela and I had just experienced the birth of our first child, Joseph Anthony. As I was putting the finishing touches on the book, we had our second son, Andrew Robert. And now, as I wrap up the work for this second cookbook, we welcome son number three, Stephen Pio. As most parents will attest, words cannot describe the joy children bring to our lives. Every day I feel blessed and eternally grateful to God that my boys are here, alive, healthy, and happy, and there is no doubt in my mind that they would not exist were it not for the gluten-free diet.

During the past few years, as I toured the country giving talks and cooking demonstrations at conferences, festivals, and support groups, I have been bombarded with similar stories about how this "simple" diet changed people's lives or the lives of their children or other family members, and also about how much they craved and missed certain foods and menu items that they could no longer eat because there were no gluten-free versions. I was moved by the stories and by the sheer number of people who e-mailed me, personally thanking me for my first book and pushing me to write a second. It was e-mails like the following from Cassandra, about her daughter Isabeau, that motivated me to write *Quick-Fix Gluten Free*:

> I wanted to extend an emphatic thank you, from myself and my five-year-old daughter, Isabeau. She has had celiac disease for the past three months. We have been trying via blogs and health stores and word of mouth to find a way for her to eat "normal" food again. Your book has had consistently excellent

recipes and lifted a huge weight off my heart. I read (after using the book for a month already) your foreword and the story of your wife. Understanding how the disease can seem to be killing someone you love, what a relief it seems at first to say, "Oh, we just can't eat gluten." However, it still brought me to tears when I saw my daughter come home from school empty-handed after one of her classmate's birthday cupcakes had been passed out. She is so stoic about it, so understanding, but the other day, I was able to give my baby a brownie again. I have to say, I was so very nervous as she took the first bite, but the joy on her face even now chokes me up. I could go on and explain how each recipe we have tried has lifted an ache from my heart and made my little "love" smile. Thank you for sharing your recipes and your story. You have made our lives richer by doing so.

    Cassandra and Isabeau

In addition to stories of hope like Cassandra and Isabeau's, I received numerous requests for hard-to-find gluten-free versions of people's favorite dishes. This book is a collection of recipes requested by all those wonderful people who wrote to me, e-mailed me, or whom I personally encountered while traveling around the country. So many of those dishes were originally made with wheat-based ingredients such as all-purpose flour and bread crumbs. Here you will find Southern-Style Chicken and Dumplings, Succulent Fried Scallops with Tartar Sauce, and beer-flavored Cheese Fondue, made entirely gluten-free. My Angela even requested a couple of her favorites from back in the day when we owned a bakery, such as Sugar-Glazed Cinnamon Rolls and Top-of-the-Morning Muffins.

In my first book I tried to cover many of the basic gluten-free cooking techniques for the person who has never cooked before, while at the same time sharing dishes that many seasoned cooks would also enjoy preparing. *Quick-Fix Gluten Free* is much the same. My dusting and encrusting techniques from *Gluten Free Every Day Cookbook* have been expanded and added to the back of this book in Techniques for Adding Flavor. You'll also find a section called The Gluten-Free Pantry that covers many of the essential gluten-free flours and ingredients, as well as a section on Understanding Gluten-Free

Flours, Doughs, and Batters. For bakers, my Pie Crust Tutorial is included in the dessert chapter to help you perfect flaky, tender, gluten-free pie crusts.

As you delve into this book, you will find recipes that can be prepped and ready to cook in 30 minutes or less. What this means is that the actual human labor involved in prepping should take less than half an hour. This does not include the necessary baking or cooking time or, for some of the baked goods, the time it takes for the dough to rise. Throughout the book, whenever extra time is needed for cooking, baking, rising, or marinating, that time is indicated near the top of the recipe. There are also helpful hints here and there for maximizing your preparation time.

The gluten-free industry has changed quite a bit over the past decade. In 2004, the industry did $560 million in sales, and at the close of 2010 it had exceeded $2 billion. The latest indicators predict that number will increase by 20 percent each year. In addition, the quality, texture, and taste of the products available are evolving and improving. Nearly every week new manufacturers, products, and brands hit the market, changing the gluten-free world. When putting together this cookbook, I tried to create dishes that could be prepared for any meal and all occasions. In many cases I mention brand names of products that I find to be of superior quality or that work perfectly in a certain dish. This doesn't mean that another brand won't work or even that I am aware of every similar product on the market, but rather that this mentioned item definitely works wonders in my own experience. That said, just be aware that one loaf of gluten-free bread may differ in taste, texture, or density from another, depending upon its ingredients, and that could change the outcome of the recipe you are preparing. I also want to assure everyone that all the ingredients I use in this book are indeed either naturally gluten free or otherwise available for purchase in a gluten-free form. It is very important when you are in the store looking for an ingredient that you read every label to ensure that you and your guests are enjoying a safe and satisfying meal.

In this book you will find recipes for breakfast and brunches such as Spinach, Bacon, and Cheddar Pie and Cinnamon-Raisin French Toast; and appetizers including Tangy Peanut Butter Chicken Skewers, Sharp Cheddar Potato Croquettes, and Savory Swedish Meatballs. There is an entire salad section with delights such as The Perfect Caesar Salad with

Herbed Croutons and a Cherry Walnut Quinoa Salad and fresh dressings made from scratch like Hearty Blue Cheese Dressing, Buttermilk Ranch Dressing, and Honey Balsamic Vinaigrette.

I included a whole bread chapter after repeated requests. There you will find Rosemary Garlic Baguettes, Grilled Pizza Crust, and Molasses Flax Sandwich Bread. And I couldn't resist doing an entire chapter called Battered and Fried, in which I share recipes for those yearned-for dishes such as Fish and Chips, Fried Mozzarella Sticks with Easy Spicy Marinara, Crispy Fried Calamari, and even Corn Dogs. In the Tasty Comforts chapter I wanted to touch on some of those classic comfort foods modified with my own personal twist, like Plum Barbecued Baby Back Ribs, Golden Walnut Baked Stuffed Shrimp, and Turkey and Tart Apple Meat Loaf. I also visited other countries and shared some international favorites such as Thai Coconut Curried Shrimp, Kickin' Paella, Shrimp Egg Rolls, and Chicken Romano.

For all of those pasta addicts out there, the Pasta and Rice chapter includes Parmesan Potato Gnocchi with Roasted Garlic Butter and Three-Cheese Penne, Pea, and Bacon Bake. And to put the perfect finishing touch on each meal, there is an entire chapter devoted to sweet treats where you'll find Chocolate and Banana Bread Pudding, Mississippi Sweet Potato Pie, Aunt Lil's Creamy Cheesecake, and Chocolate-Espresso Cookies. This is just a short list of the many easy-to-make, flavorful, and safe-to-eat dishes you'll discover in *Quick-Fix Gluten Free*. I am thrilled to have had the opportunity to share this culinary adventure with you all!

1  Peter H.R. Green, M.D., and Rory Jones. *Celiac Disease: A Hidden Epidemic* (New York: HarperCollins, 2006 ), 21–22.

2  Dr. Stephen Wangen, *Healthier Without Wheat* (Seattle: Innate Health Publishing, 2009), 22–23.

## Speeding Up Your Preparation Time

During my years in culinary school, the term *mise en place* was used constantly. It means "everything in place," or that as student chefs we had better have everything set up and ready to go before actually beginning any recipe. This mantra is one that I continue to live by. Before starting any dish, always make sure you have everything, including measured ingredients, equipment, counter, oven, and refrigerator space, ready. There is nothing worse than being halfway through a recipe and having to dismantle the kitchen to find a missing measuring spoon or casserole dish or realizing that you have only two eggs when the recipe calls for three. Despite the fact that I have authored two cookbooks and worked in commercial settings, I will admit that my own kitchen is probably a lot like one found in the average home. I still need my measuring spoons and whisks, and I often find myself searching the entire house or backyard, only to find them in the sandbox (they apparently are cool sand toys) or being used as microphones for Joseph and Andrew's concerts. Having to find such items during the cooking process will definitely add to your preparation time! To prevent this I always take the easy step of first reading the entire recipe from beginning to end. Second, I do an ingredient check to make sure I have everything I need, in the right proportions and at my fingertips. Then I pull out all the required equipment. Another way to save time and reduce stress when making a particular dish for breakfast or a big gathering is to try to accomplish as much of the prep work as possible the night before. That way, close to mealtime, all I have to do is assemble and cook the recipe. Some of the recipes include tips for prepping ahead of time and sometimes even refrigerating or freezing things for later use.

## Kitchen Equipment

You will find that the recipes in this book do not require any out-of-the-ordinary or over-the-top cooking utensils or equipment. Many people believe a chef must own every unique kitchen gadget known to man, and this is far from the truth. The recipes in this book require only basic utensils such as measuring spoons and cups, cutting boards and knives, mixing bowls, pots and pans, a rolling pin, wooden spoons, whisks, tongs, and spatulas. The cooking equipment that I strongly recommend to optimize your time and make your life a bit easier includes an electric stand or hand mixer, a basic food processor, a blender, a positive attitude, and most important, a glass filled with your favorite gluten-free beer or wine.

# quick-fix
## gluten free

# morning glories

Breakfast is often my favorite meal of the day. There is something about the aroma of crisp bacon, scrambled eggs, and sweet waffles that makes me want to jump out of bed, excited to begin a new day. For me, the ideal breakfast starts (and continues) with a good cup of steaming coffee, one that can be refilled and enjoyed many times throughout the day. Fortunately, for those with celiac disease, most coffees and many teas are gluten free and safe to consume on a daily basis. The same can be said for eggs and bacon and most packaged sausages, as long as one reads the labels and determines that all the ingredients and fillers are gluten free. This doesn't, however, hold true for most of the other morning staples, which have always screamed "breakfast time!" right at me. I am thinking of a big stack of buttermilk pancakes served with melted butter and syrup, sumptuous French toast dusted with confectioners' sugar, or waffles topped with strawberries and whipped cream. These are just a few examples of signature breakfast items of which I have developed gluten-free versions for this chapter, to bring back to you what you thought might be gone forever.

During the nineties, my wife and I owned a bakery café called the Sugar Shack. We were known for miles around for our fresh and delicious pastries and muffins. People would line up at the counter to order cinnamon rolls hot out of the oven and oozing with brown sugar and walnuts in a sweet sugar glaze, or a Very Berry Muffin packed with fresh blueberries, raspberries, and blackberries, or the Top-of-the-Morning Muffins packed with apples, carrots, coconut, and a blend of sugar and spices. When Angela was diagnosed with celiac disease in 2000, we reluctantly decided to sell the business. Many times afterward, Angela would wistfully relate how much she missed some of those incredible treats. With that in mind, I decided to go back in time and break out that old three-ring binder stuffed with those classic Sugar Shack recipes. After testing and tweaking, and altering a few of the ingredients (primarily changing the blends of flours), we are now able to share with everyone some of these beloved bakery delights. I hope that this chapter will motivate you all to jump out of bed, head to the kitchen, and start your day out just right!

# belgian waffles

## makes 6 to 8 servings

Flaxseed meal gives these waffles a nutty flavor and whole-grain appeal, and yet they are still the same chewy, delicious Saturday morning breakfast treat that kids love. Top with berries and whipped cream for a special start to the weekend!

½ cup tapioca flour
¼ cup corn flour
¼ cup white rice flour
2 tablespoons flaxseed meal
2 tablespoons brown sugar
1 teaspoon baking soda
½ teaspoon ground cinnamon
½ teaspoon salt
¼ teaspoon baking powder

3 eggs, separated
1 cup buttermilk
1 teaspoon vanilla extract
3 tablespoons unsalted butter, melted
Maple syrup, for serving
Fresh strawberries, for serving (optional)
Fresh blueberries, for serving (optional)
Whipped cream, for serving (optional)

Preheat a waffle iron.

In a medium bowl, whisk together the tapioca flour, corn flour, white rice flour, flaxseed meal, brown sugar, baking soda, cinnamon, salt, and baking powder. Set aside.

In a large bowl, whisk together the egg yolks, buttermilk, vanilla, and melted butter.

Slowly mix the dry ingredients into the wet ingredients until completely incorporated. Set the batter aside.

Using an electric mixer, whip the egg whites in a bowl until soft peaks form. Using a spatula, fold the egg whites into the batter until blended.

Spray the waffle iron grids with nonstick cooking spray and then ladle the batter into the grid until covered. Close the lid and cook for 2 to 3 minutes, until golden brown. Place the waffles on a platter, keeping it warm in a warm oven if desired, and serve with syrup, strawberries, blueberries, and whipped cream.

# buttermilk pancakes

## makes 4 servings

When I ask my son Joseph, "What do you want for breakfast?" he invariably yells, "Pancakes!" Now, with this light and fluffy gluten-free version, everyone will want to join in that chorus. Make them unique for each individual by adding ingredients like chocolate chips, blueberries, butterscotch chips, bananas, or walnuts to each pancake as it cooks and watch the pancakes disappear!

½ cup tapioca flour
¼ cup corn flour
¼ cup white rice flour
1 teaspoon baking powder
2 tablespoons flaxseed meal
1 teaspoon granulated sugar

¾ cup buttermilk
1 egg
1 tablespoon vegetable oil
1 teaspoon vanilla extract
Maple syrup, for serving

In a medium bowl, sift together the tapioca flour, corn flour, white rice flour, and baking powder. Whisk in the flaxseed meal and sugar and set aside.

In a separate bowl, whisk together the buttermilk, egg, vegetable oil, and vanilla.

Add the dry ingredients to the wet ingredients and whisk until just incorporated.

Heat a large nonstick skillet over medium heat. Gently ladle ¼ cup batter into the pan and cook for 2 to 3 minutes, until golden brown. Flip over and cook until the second side is set and golden brown. Transfer to a platter, keeping it warm in a warm oven if desired, and repeat with the rest of the batter. Serve with maple syrup.

chef's note: After ladling the batter into the pan to make a pancake, try adding blueberries, chocolate chips, bananas, or any other favorite pancake mix-ins.

# cinnamon-raisin french toast

## makes 4 servings

This recipe was created in response to a special request from an autism support group of dedicated moms trying to find a few gluten- and dairy-free foods that would be enticing enough for their children to want to eat. This cinnamon-dusted French toast was an instant crowd-pleaser and made a few of those beautiful children smile.

1 cup milk or nondairy alternative (page 180)
1 teaspoon granulated sugar
¼ teaspoon salt
¼ teaspoon ground cinnamon
3 eggs

3 tablespoons butter or nondairy alternative (page 180)
12 slices Udi's Cinnamon Raisin Bread
Confectioners' sugar, for serving
Maple syrup, for serving

In a medium bowl, whisk together the milk, granulated sugar, salt, cinnamon, and eggs.

Melt the butter in a large nonstick skillet over medium heat.

Dredge the bread in the egg mixture for 20 to 30 seconds, coating both sides.

Allow the excess egg to completely drip off the bread before placing it in the pan and cooking for 1 to 2 minutes, until golden brown on both sides.

Place the French toast on a platter, keeping it warm in a warm oven if desired, and repeat with the remaining bread. Dust the French toast with confectioners' sugar and serve with maple syrup.

# top-of-the-morning muffins

## makes 12

## baking time: 25 to 30 minutes

Chock-full of walnuts, raisins, carrot, coconut, and applesauce, these spiced muffins are the best thing since sliced bread! My wife's secret splurge is to top them with cream cheese or frosting.

½ cup sorghum flour
½ cup brown rice flour
½ cup white rice flour
¼ cup tapioca flour
1 teaspoon xanthan gum
1 teaspoon baking soda
½ teaspoon salt
1 teaspoon plus ⅛ teaspoon ground cinnamon
¼ teaspoon ground ginger
¼ teaspoon ground nutmeg

8 tablespoons (1 stick) butter, at room temperature
½ cup plus 1 tablespoon granulated sugar
½ cup packed brown sugar
½ cup applesauce
2 eggs, beaten
1 cup shredded carrots
½ cup walnuts
⅓ cup shredded sweetened coconut
¼ cup raisins

Preheat the oven to 350°F and grease a 12-cup muffin tin.

In a medium bowl, sift together the sorghum flour, brown rice flour, white rice flour, and tapioca flour. Whisk in the xanthan gum, baking soda, salt, 1 teaspoon of the cinnamon, the ginger, and the nutmeg. Set aside.

Using an electric mixer, cream together the butter, ½ cup of the granulated sugar, and the brown sugar until light and fluffy. Beat in the applesauce and eggs and then gradually blend in the dry ingredients until a smooth batter forms. Mix in the carrots, walnuts, coconut, and raisins. Fill the prepared muffin tins two-thirds full. For the topping, mix together the remaining 1 tablespoon sugar and ⅛ teaspoon cinnamon. Sprinkle the muffins with the cinnamon sugar and bake for 25 to 30 minutes, until a toothpick inserted in the center of a muffin comes out clean. Remove from the oven and allow to cool in the pan before unmolding and serving.

# very berry muffins

## makes 12

### baking time: 25 to 30 minutes

These sweet and soft gluten-free muffins are a triple-berry delight. Serve with a steaming cup of coffee for a Sunday morning treat.

½ cup sorghum flour
½ cup brown rice flour
½ cup white rice flour
¼ cup tapioca flour
1½ teaspoons baking powder
1 teaspoon xanthan gum
½ teaspoon salt
6 tablespoons butter, at room temperature

½ cup plus 1 tablespoon granulated sugar
½ cup packed brown sugar
½ cup milk
1 egg
1½ cups mixed fresh or frozen berries (raspberries, blueberries, and blackberries)

Preheat the oven to 350°F and grease a 12-cup muffin tin.

In a medium bowl, sift together the sorghum flour, brown rice flour, white rice flour, and tapioca flour. Whisk in the baking powder, xanthan gum, and salt. Set aside.

Using an electric mixer, cream together the butter, ½ cup of the granulated sugar, and the brown sugar until light and fluffy. Beat in the milk and egg and then gradually blend in the dry ingredients until a smooth batter forms. Fold in the mixed berries and then fill the prepared muffin tins two-thirds full. Sprinkle the muffins with the remaining 1 tablespoon sugar and bake for 25 to 30 minutes, until a toothpick inserted into the center of a muffin comes out clean. Remove from the oven and allow to cool in the pan before unmolding and serving.

# the ultimate breakfast cookie

## makes 5 dozen

### baking time: 12 to 14 minutes

I can't count the number of times I've told my kids that they can't have cookies for breakfast. This changed when we perfected these delicious, flourless, healthy cookies—filled with oats, nuts, seeds, and banana. They are a high-fiber, protein-packed alternative to the morning toaster pastry or doughnut.

4½ cups gluten-free oats
2 teaspoons baking soda
½ cup flaxseed meal
1½ cups natural peanut butter
8 tablespoons (1 stick) butter, at room temperature
1 cup packed brown sugar
¾ cup granulated sugar
¼ cup honey

1 banana, mashed
3 eggs, beaten
1 teaspoon vanilla extract
¾ cup sliced almonds, chopped
¾ cup miniature chocolate chips
½ teaspoon roasted unsalted sunflower seeds

Preheat the oven to 350°F.

In a medium bowl, combine the oats, baking soda, and flaxseed meal.

Using an electric mixer, cream together the peanut butter, butter, brown sugar, granulated sugar, honey, and banana in another bowl. Beat in the eggs and vanilla and then slowly add the oat mixture until thoroughly mixed. Stir in the almonds, chocolate chips, and sunflower seeds.

Drop tablespoonfuls of dough 2 inches apart on ungreased cookie sheets. Bake for 12 to 14 minutes, until golden brown, and then cool on the pans.

chef's note: For an even healthier version, substitute dried fruit such as apples, dates, or figs for the chocolate chips.

# sugar-glazed cinnamon rolls

## makes 12

### rising time: 1 hour

### baking time: 15 to 20 minutes

Imagine a life where you could never again wake up to the incredible scent of baking cinnamon rolls. I firmly believe that this should never happen, so I came up with this sticky, sweet, and chewy gluten-free version made with tapioca flour, flaxseed meal, and walnuts. You will love these cinnamon rolls!

½ cup buttermilk
¼ cup apple cider or juice
¼ cup granulated sugar
1 tablespoon active dry yeast
1¼ cups tapioca flour, plus more for dusting
1 cup brown rice flour
¼ cup potato starch
¼ cup flaxseed meal
2½ teaspoons xanthan gum
2 teaspoons baking powder
½ teaspoon salt
¼ teaspoon baking soda
¼ teaspoon ground cinnamon
2 tablespoons butter, melted
2 tablespoons vegetable oil
1 egg plus 1 egg white
1 teaspoon vanilla extract

**Filling**

½ cup packed brown sugar
¼ cup granulated sugar
1 tablespoon ground cinnamon
4 tablespoons (½ stick) butter, melted
¼ cup chopped walnuts

**Glaze**

¾ cup confectioners' sugar
1½ tablespoons milk
½ teaspoon vanilla extract

To make the dough: In a small saucepan or microwave-safe bowl, whisk together the buttermilk and cider. Warm the mixture to 110°F, add the granulated sugar, and sprinkle the yeast on top. Set aside.

In a large bowl, whisk together the tapioca flour, brown rice flour, potato starch, flaxseed meal, xanthan gum, baking powder, salt, baking soda, and cinnamon. Add the butter, oil, egg, egg white, vanilla, and yeast mixture, stirring until thoroughly combined. The dough will be sticky. Remove from the mixing bowl and place in a greased large bowl. Cover with plastic wrap, put in a warm place, and allow to rise for 1 hour, or until doubled in bulk.

Meanwhile, begin preparing the filling: Whisk together the brown sugar, granulated sugar, and cinnamon, and set aside. Grease a 12-cup muffin tin and set aside.

When the dough has risen, dust a sheet of wax paper with tapioca flour and place the dough on top. Sprinkle the top of the dough with more tapioca flour and place another sheet or two of wax paper on top. Roll out the dough into a 15 by 10-inch rectangle. Remove the top sheets of wax paper and coat the entire exposed surface with the 4 tablespoons of melted butter. Sprinkle the sugar filling mixture evenly over the butter, followed by the walnuts. Then, using the bottom piece of wax paper on the 15-inch side, slowly roll the dough away from you into the shape of a log or jelly roll, pinching the seams together. It is important to roll slowly with one hand while using the other to assist in peeling the dough away from the wax paper, as it may stick. Use a sharp knife to cut 12 even slices about 1 inch thick and place them cut side down into the muffin cups. Cover with a clean dish towel, place in a warm spot, and allow to rise for 1 hour, until the dough reaches the top of the muffin tins.

Preheat the oven to 375°F. Bake for 15 to 20 minutes, until golden brown. While the cinnamon rolls are cooling, make the glaze by whisking together the confectioners' sugar, milk, and vanilla in a small bowl. After the cinnamon rolls have cooled for 20 minutes, drizzle with the glaze. Run the edge of a knife around each cinnamon roll and transfer them to a serving platter.

# sweet cheese crêpes with caramelized peaches and granola

## makes 4 to 6 servings

These delectable crêpes teeming with sweetly caramelized peaches and crunchy granola were rated highly enough to grace the cover of this cookbook.

½ cup white rice flour
¼ cup tapioca flour
¼ cup cornstarch
½ teaspoon xanthan gum
2 teaspoons granulated sugar
½ teaspoon salt
1½ cups milk
6 tablespoons water

3 eggs
4 tablespoons (½ stick) butter,
    2 tablespoons melted
1 teaspoon vanilla extract
Sweet Cheese Filling (recipe follows)
Peach Topping (recipe follows)
½ cup "Gone Completely Nuts" Granola
    (page 19)

In a small bowl, sift together the white rice flour, tapioca flour, cornstarch, xanthan gum, granulated sugar, and salt.

In a blender, combine the milk, water, eggs, melted butter, and vanilla. Blend for 10 seconds. Add the flour mixture and blend for another 30 to 40 seconds, until it forms a smooth batter.

Heat a nonstick pan over medium heat. Spray with nonstick cooking spray, pour about 2 tablespoons of batter in the center, and swirl the pan in a circular motion so the batter forms a thin disk. Cook for 50 to 60 seconds, then use a spatula to flip the disk and cook for another 10 to 15 seconds. Place the disk on a sheet of wax paper to cool and continue making crêpes with the remaining batter, stacking them between sheets of wax paper.

When all the crêpes have cooled, spread 1 to 1½ tablespoons of the cheese filling on half of a crêpe. Fold the crêpe in half once and then in half a second time, forming a triangular envelope. Place on a platter and continue to fill the rest of the crêpes.

Melt 1 tablespoon of the remaining butter in a large nonstick pan over medium heat. Add half of the crêpes and cook for 1 to 2 minutes, until light golden brown. Flip and cook for another minute. Place the cooked crêpes on a platter and cook the remaining crêpes in the remaining 1 tablespoon butter.

To serve, divide the crêpes among four to six plates and top each serving with a spoonful of peach topping and a sprinkle of granola.

**chef's note:** To save time, cook the unfilled crêpes in advance and store them stacked between layers of wax paper in resealable plastic bags. They can be refrigerated for 2 to 3 days or frozen for 3 to 4 weeks.

## sweet cheese filling

1 (8-ounce) package cream cheese,
   at room temperature
2 tablespoons brown sugar

½ teaspoon ground cinnamon
½ teaspoon ground nutmeg

Using an electric mixer with a paddle, beat together the cream cheese, brown sugar, cinnamon, and nutmeg until smooth and creamy.

## peach topping

1 tablespoon butter
1 pound frozen sliced peaches,
   thawed and slices cut in half

2 tablespoons brown sugar
⅛ teaspoon ground cinnamon

Melt the butter in a large skillet over medium heat. Add the peaches, brown sugar, and cinnamon and cook, stirring occasionally, until the peaches are softened and their juices are released, about 5 minutes.

# spinach, bacon, and cheddar pie

## makes 1 (9-inch) pie

## baking time: 50 to 55 minutes

This egg pie has many similarities to quiche but is lighter and fluffier. Its classic savory combination of bacon, cheddar cheese, and fresh baby spinach baked into an irresistible crust guarantees it will be a Sunday brunch favorite. See the pie crust tutorial (page 144) for tips on making gluten-free crusts.

### Cheddar Pie Crust

1¼ cups white rice flour
1 cup tapioca flour
1 tablespoon granulated sugar
½ teaspoon baking soda
½ teaspoon xanthan gum
½ teaspoon salt
¼ cup vegetable shortening
¼ cup shredded cheddar or Swiss cheese
4 tablespoons (½ stick) butter, cold
½ cup milk

### Filling

1 cup packed baby spinach
½ pound bacon, cooked until crisp and crumbled
5 eggs, beaten
1¼ cups light cream or half-and half
1½ cups grated sharp yellow cheddar or Swiss cheese
Pinch of salt
Pinch of freshly ground black pepper

To make the crust: In a medium bowl, whisk together the white rice flour, tapioca flour, sugar, baking soda, xanthan gum, and salt. Add the shortening, cheese, and butter to the flour mixture.

Using your fingertips, a pastry blender, or two butter knives, rub or cut the shortening and butter into the dry ingredients until they are the texture of a coarse meal, with pea-size pieces. Gradually stir in the milk with a fork to moisten the dry ingredients. Using your hands, form the dough into a ball and wrap in plastic wrap. Refrigerate for 2 hours or up to 1 week.

Roll the dough into a 12-inch round between 2 sheets of wax paper. Remove the wax paper from the top of the round and invert the pie plate on top of the dough. Place your other hand under the wax paper and turn the round over so that the dough falls into the pan. Gently tuck the dough into the pan and then peel off the wax paper. Let the excess dough drape over the edge of the pie plate, while gently fitting the dough into the pan. Using a knife, cut the excess dough away from the edge of the pie plate. Use your fingers to crimp the edges.

Preheat the oven to 350°F.

To fill the crust: Layer the spinach and bacon in the bottom of the unbaked crust.

In a large bowl, whisk together the eggs, light cream, cheese, salt, and pepper. Pour on top of the spinach and bacon. Cover the pie crust edges with aluminum foil to prevent overbrowning. Bake for 50 to 55 minutes, until a knife inserted in the center comes out clean and the crust is golden brown, removing the foil after the first 20 minutes. Allow to rest for 10 minutes, then cut into 8 wedges and serve.

# blueberry and cream cheese french toast strata

## makes 6 to 8 servings

### baking time: 1 hour

This is really a French toast casserole, made with blueberries and decadent cream cheese baked with eggs, cream, and bread and seasoned with vanilla, cinnamon, nutmeg, and sugar. Drizzle with maple syrup before serving and watch your guests fight over the last piece!

1 (12-ounce) loaf Udi's White Sandwich or Whole Grain Bread, cut into 1-inch cubes
6 ounces cream cheese, cubed
1 cup (6 ounces) fresh or drained thawed frozen blueberries
8 eggs
1¾ cups whole milk or heavy whipping cream

¼ cup maple syrup, plus more for drizzling
4 tablespoons (½ stick) butter, melted
½ teaspoon vanilla extract
½ teaspoon ground cinnamon
⅛ teaspoon ground nutmeg
Confectioners' sugar, for dusting

Grease an 11 by 7-inch baking dish. Place half the bread cubes in the dish, followed by the cream cheese cubes and the blueberries. Top with the remaining bread cubes.

In a medium bowl, whisk together the eggs, milk, ¼ cup of the syrup, the melted butter, vanilla, cinnamon, and nutmeg. Pour evenly over the bread, cover with aluminum foil, and refrigerate for 1 hour.

Preheat the oven to 325°F and bake, covered, for 30 minutes. Remove the foil and bake for another 25 to 30 minutes, until the center is set and the edges are golden brown. Let stand for 10 minutes before cutting and serving, dusted with confectioners' sugar and drizzled with maple syrup.

# "gone completely nuts" granola

## makes 1½ pounds

## baking time: 1 hour

Brimming with nuts, honey, cranberries, and coconut, this granola is a high-energy snack, fit for any mountain biker, snowboarder, or long-distance hiker. It's also pretty good when you are just sitting on the couch and watching a movie . . .

¼ cup maple syrup
2 tablespoons honey
1 tablespoon vegetable oil
3 cups gluten-free oats
½ cup chopped walnuts
½ cup chopped pecans
½ cup chopped almonds

½ cup lightly packed shredded sweetened coconut
¼ cup packed brown sugar
½ teaspoon salt
1 cup dried cranberries or cherries
½ cup raisins (optional)

Preheat the oven to 250°F and grease a baking sheet.

In a small bowl, whisk together the maple syrup, honey, and vegetable oil. In a medium mixing bowl, combine the oats, walnuts, pecans, almonds, coconut, brown sugar, and salt. Add the syrup mixture to the oat mixture and, using an electric mixer, mix until thoroughly blended.

Spread out evenly on the baking pan and bake for 1 hour, stirring every 20 minutes. Allow to cool completely on the pan and then mix in the dried cranberries and raisins. Store in an airtight container or resealable plastic bag for up to 2 weeks.

# maple-glazed grilled fruit skewers

## makes 4 servings

## marinating time: 1 to 3 hours

What an awesome way to get your daily requirement of fruit! These skewered chunks of pineapple, nectarines, plums, and peaches are dripping with a vanilla, nutmeg, cinnamon, and maple syrup. Serve as a dessert at the end of that Sunday brunch.

½ cup maple syrup
1 teaspoon vanilla extract
¼ teaspoon ground nutmeg
⅛ teaspoon ground cinnamon
2 firm peaches, halved and pitted
2 firm plums, halved and pitted

2 firm nectarines, halved and pitted
1 cup pineapple chunks
4 wooden skewers, soaked in water for
   20 minutes
1 pint vanilla ice cream or nondairy
   substitute

In a medium bowl, whisk together the maple syrup, vanilla, nutmeg, and cinnamon. Add the fruit and toss gently to coat with the glaze. Refrigerate for at least 1 hour and up to 3 hours. Preheat a grill to medium-high and generously oil the grates. Thread the fruit on the skewers, alternating varieties. Place the skewered fruit on the grill, cut side down, and cook for 2 to 3 minutes per side, until heated through and caramelized. Place each skewer on a plate and serve with a scoop of vanilla ice cream.

# maple-drizzled fruit salad
# with toasted coconut

## makes 4 servings

## baking time: 1 hour

This maple-drizzled salad made with pineapple, cantaloupe, honeydew, and grapes is an awesome alternative to the drab morning banana. You can also whip this up as a light and nutritious lunch.

½ cup vanilla yogurt
2 tablespoons maple syrup
½ cup pineapple cubes
½ cup halved grapes
½ cup cantaloupe cubes

½ cup honeydew melon cubes
1 tablespoon finely chopped fresh mint
¼ cup grated fresh coconut, toasted
   (page 182)

In small bowl, whisk together the yogurt and syrup and set aside.

In a medium bowl, toss together the pineapple, grapes, cantaloupe, honeydew, and mint.

Place the fruit in four martini glasses with a dollop of yogurt and a sprinkle of toasted coconut.

# chapter 2

# teasers

Feta-Zucchini Medallions
  with Lemon-Garlic Yogurt Sauce   25

Bacon-Wrapped Dates Stuffed
  with Almonds and Goat Cheese   26

Savory Swedish Meatballs   27

Blue Cheese and Spinach–Stuffed Mushrooms   28

Garlicky Herbed Cheese Spread   29

Sweet and Spicy Korean Fried Chicken Wings   30

Sesame-Coconut Onion Rings
  with Orange Marmalade Dipping Sauce   31

Grilled Antipasto Platter   32

Tangy Peanut Butter Chicken Skewers   33

Arancini (Rice Balls with Cheese)   34

Spinach Parmesan Bites
  with Honey Mustard Dipping Sauce   35

Sharp Cheddar Potato Croquettes   36

Cheesy Crab, Spinach, and Artichoke Dip   37

Hors d'oeuvres are typically fun, flavorful, teasing parcels of food made to go with a fantastic glass of wine, good friends, and conversation. Our friends Denise and Mike are big fans of these little culinary delights. When they go out to a restaurant, the two of them prefer to order and split three or four appetizers in lieu of a heavy or expensive entrée. This way they enjoy a large variety of creative dishes and walk away happy and satisfied without feeling overstuffed.

Over the years Angela and I have done our share of entertaining, preparing feasts for birthdays, holidays, anniversaries, and other occasions. Many times our guests have commented that they love coming to dinner at our home because a unique and incredible appetizer is always served before the meal. At times they've tried something they have never tasted or even heard of before. Often we'll end up thinking everyone would have been just as happy, and maybe even more relaxed, milling around and socializing while munching on hors d'oeuvres instead of sitting down for a formal dinner.

For those with celiac disease, cheese and gluten-free crackers have become a premeal mainstay, so enhancing and expanding this repertoire became my focal point for this chapter. At your next party, how about setting up appetizer stations that offer Savory Swedish Meatballs or a Cheesy Crab, Spinach, and Artichoke Dip to shake things up? And for your guests who crave those classic pub appetizers, hand them a plate of the Sweet and Spicy Korean Fried Chicken Wings or my Sesame-Coconut Onion Rings with Orange Marmalade Dipping Sauce and see if that makes them happy. This chapter also offers recipes for Blue Cheese and Spinach–Stuffed Mushrooms, Spinach Parmesan Bites with Honey Mustard Dipping Sauce, and Sharp Cheddar Potato Croquettes— guaranteed to satisfy and convert any die-hard fan of the standard cheese-and-crackers appetizer.

# feta-zucchini medallions with lemon-garlic yogurt sauce

## makes 4 to 6 servings

This is a vegetable lover's delight, using lots of squash, a bit of feta, and a small amount of rice flour to create a light and delicious snack complemented by lemon yogurt.

2 medium zucchini (about ¾ pound)
2 medium yellow squash (about ¾ pound)
1 cup gluten-free bread crumbs
¾ cup crumbled feta cheese (about 4 ounces)
¼ cup minced Vidalia or other sweet onion
2 tablespoons white rice flour
1 tablespoon finely chopped fresh dill

½ teaspoon salt
¼ teaspoon freshly ground black pepper
1 egg, beaten
2 tablespoons unsalted butter, or more as needed
2 tablespoons vegetable oil, or more as needed
Lemon-Garlic Yogurt Sauce (recipe follows)

Using a grater, grate the zucchini and squash into a medium bowl.

Transfer to a strainer and press out extra liquid; transfer back to the dried bowl.

Mix in the bread crumbs, feta cheese, onion, white rice flour, dill, salt, pepper, and egg.

Using your hands, form and shape the batter into 2-inch patties.

In a medium skillet over medium heat, melt the butter and vegetable oil.

Cook the patties for 3 to 4 minutes per side, until golden brown, adding more butter and oil when needed.

Place the patties on a platter with a dollop of the sauce on each.

## lemon-garlic yogurt sauce (makes ¾ cup)

6 ounces Greek yogurt
2 cloves garlic, chopped

1 teaspoon freshly squeezed lemon juice
⅛ teaspoon cayenne

Place all the ingredients in a small food processor and blend until thoroughly combined. Refrigerate until needed. Stored in an airtight container, it will keep in the refrigerator for up to 2 days.

# bacon-wrapped dates stuffed with almonds and goat cheese

## makes 2 dozen

A full palette of flavors converges here with the sweet dates complemented by the smoky bacon, creamy goat cheese, and nutty almonds.

**24 large pitted dates (preferably Medjool)**
**24 unsalted roasted almonds**

**2 ounces goat cheese**
**12 strips bacon, halved crosswise**

Preheat the oven to 400°F and grease a baking pan.

Cut a lengthwise slit in each date and stuff with an almond. Using a spoon or a pastry bag, fill each date with ½ teaspoon goat cheese. Squeeze the dates shut and wrap tightly in bacon, using a toothpick to secure each date shut. Place the dates on the baking pan seam side down and cook until the bacon is crispy, about 10 minutes, turning the cooked dates over halfway through cooking. Remove from the oven, allow the dates to cool, and serve at room temperature.

# savory swedish meatballs

## makes 30 to 40

Norway, Finland, and Denmark all have their own versions of this smorgasbord specialty that originated in Sweden. Now comes the gluten-free adaptation from a small town in Connecticut, using white rice flour and small pieces of Udi's bread kneaded into ground pork and beef, blended with spices, and topped with red currant jelly. You won't care what country they came from!

3 slices Udi's White Sandwich Bread, cut into small pieces
¼ cup half-and-half
2 tablespoons plus 1 tablespoon unsalted butter
½ cup minced onion
1 pound ground beef
1 pound ground pork
2 eggs, beaten

1 teaspoon kosher salt
½ teaspoon ground allspice
¼ teaspoon freshly ground black pepper
¼ teaspoon dry mustard
¼ teaspoon ground nutmeg
2 tablespoons white rice flour
2 cups beef broth
¼ cup sour cream
2 tablespoons red currant jelly

In a small bowl, combine the bread and half-and-half and set aside.

In a medium skillet over medium heat, melt 1 tablespoon of the butter. Add the onion and cook, stirring occasionally, for 3 to 4 minutes, until tender.

Using a stand mixer with the paddle attachment, or a handheld electric mixer, beat together the beef, pork, eggs, salt, allspice, pepper, dry mustard, nutmeg, cooked onion, and bread-milk mixture for 1 minute on medium speed.

Using a tablespoon measure, scoop out the meat mixture and shape into 1¼-inch meatballs with your hands.

Heat the remaining 2 tablespoons of the butter in a large skillet over medium heat and add the meatballs without crowding the pan.

Cook the meatballs, turning occasionally, for 8 to 10 minutes, until golden brown on all sides. Transfer the cooked meatballs to a baking dish and keep warm in a warm oven while you cook the rest of the meatballs.

After all the meatballs have been cooked, add the white rice flour to the pan and whisk for 2 minutes to blend the flour into the drippings in the pan. Slowly add the beef broth and continue whisking until the sauce begins to thicken and becomes smooth, 3 to 4 minutes. Whisk in the sour cream and jelly and simmer until the sauce is creamy and coats the back of a spoon.

Place the meatballs in a serving dish and pour the gravy over the top.

# blue cheese and spinach–stuffed mushrooms

## makes 40

These stuffed mushrooms have become a holiday must-have in our home. Serve them hot out of the oven and watch from the corner of your eye as people walk by and stealthily pop one right after another.

1½ cups hot gluten-free chicken broth
2½ cups (about 6 ounces) Aleia's Savory Stuffing mix
1 (10-ounce) package frozen spinach, thawed, drained, and squeezed dry

40 medium mushrooms (about 2 pounds)
2 tablespoons butter
2 cloves garlic, minced
¼ pound blue cheese
½ cup finely grated Parmesan cheese

Preheat the oven to 400°F and grease a baking pan.

In a large bowl, stir the chicken broth into the stuffing mix until moistened. Set aside for 5 minutes; then add the spinach.

Remove the stems from the mushrooms and dice the stems.

In a skillet over medium-high heat, melt the butter. Add the mushroom stems and garlic and cook, stirring occasionally, for about 5 minutes, until tender. Add to the stuffing mixture along with the blue cheese and Parmesan and mix until thoroughly incorporated.

Spoon the mixture into the mushroom caps, place in the baking pan, and bake for about 15 minutes, until cooked through.

chef's note: Some varieties of blue cheese may contain wheat and gluten. Make sure you read labels to avoid contamination. The mushrooms can be made 1 day ahead and refrigerated until ready to bake.

# garlicky herbed cheese spread

## makes 1½ cups

Finding a quick, easy, and delicious appetizer that can be enjoyed by all is not a simple task. This super garlicky herbed cheese is fantastic on gluten-free crackers or spread on a roast beef sandwich.

2 cloves garlic
⅛ teaspoon salt
8 tablespoons (1 stick) butter, at room temperature
1 (8-ounce) package Neufchâtel cheese, at room temperature

½ teaspoon dried oregano
⅛ teaspoon dried thyme leaves
⅛ teaspoon dried marjoram leaves
⅛ teaspoon dried dill
⅛ teaspoon freshly ground black pepper

Mince the garlic on a cutting board, sprinkle with the salt, and using the flat side of the knife, crush the garlic until a paste forms.

With an electric mixer, beat together the butter, Neufchâtel cheese, garlic paste, oregano, thyme, marjoram, dill, and black pepper.

Place the mixture in a bowl and serve, or refrigerate the cheese until needed and bring to room temperature before serving.

# sweet and spicy korean fried chicken wings

## makes 6 servings

### marinating time: 3 hours or overnight

I recently attended a potluck dinner at a family reunion. Four different pans of chicken wings were set upon the banquet table by four different cooks. These sweet and spicy fried wings were the first to go, leaving the others to sit in their sauce.

1 cup milk
2 tablespoons granulated sugar
2 teaspoons salt
1 teaspoon freshly ground black pepper
½ teaspoon ground ginger
3 pounds chicken wings
¾ cup white rice flour
¼ cup potato starch
1½ tablespoons curry powder

¼ cup minced sweet onion
1 tablespoon olive oil
⅓ cup tomato sauce
½ cup sweet red chili sauce
½ cup water
1 tablespoon gluten-free Worcestershire sauce
Vegetable oil, for deep frying
2 green onions, finely chopped

In a large bowl, whisk together the milk, sugar, salt, pepper, and ginger. Add the chicken wings and marinate in the refrigerator for at least 3 hours or overnight.

In a medium bowl, whisk together the white rice flour, potato starch, and curry powder. Set aside.

In a medium saucepan over medium heat, cook the sweet onion in the olive oil, stirring, until soft, about 3 minutes. Stir in the tomato sauce, chili sauce, water, and Worcestershire sauce. Simmer until the sauce thickens slightly, about 5 minutes; set aside.

In a large saucepan, heat 3 inches of vegetable oil until a deep-fat thermometer

reads 350°F. Drain the chicken wings in a colander while the oil heats.

Toss 6 to 8 chicken wings at a time into the seasoned flour and then slowly add them to the hot oil, precooking the wings for 4 to 5 minutes, until lightly golden. Remove from the hot oil with tongs or a slotted spoon and place on paper towels to cool. Continue until all the wings are precooked.

Increase the temperature of the oil to 375°F and cook 6 to 8 chicken wings at once a second time for 4 to 5 minutes, until golden brown and crispy. Place the cooked wings in a large bowl, ladle with sauce, and toss until completely coated. Place on a platter and sprinkle with green onions.

# sesame-coconut onion rings with orange marmalade dipping sauce

## makes 6 servings

The onion rings in my first cookbook were such a big hit that I vowed to come up with an even better variation. After much experimentation with new flours and batter mixes, I stumbled upon the perfect combination of white rice, almond meal, coconut, and beer. The batter clings to the tender onions with a unique and sweet hint of coconut and the nutty flavor of sesame seeds. Slather these onion rings with the orange marmalade and honey mustard dipping sauce for a truly special flavor sensation.

¾ cup white rice flour
¼ cup almond meal flour
¾ cup finely shredded sweetened coconut
2 tablespoons sesame seeds
1 teaspoon salt
¼ teaspoon cayenne

2 egg yolks
¾ cup gluten-free beer
Vegetable oil, for deep frying
2 sweet yellow onions, cut into ½-inch rings
Orange Marmalade Dipping Sauce
   (recipe follows)

In a medium bowl, whisk together the white rice flour, almond meal, coconut, sesame seeds, salt, and cayenne. Gradually whisk in the egg yolks and beer until a smooth batter forms.

In a large saucepan, heat 3 inches of vegetable oil until a deep-fat thermometer reads 360°F. Dip a few onions at a time into the batter and then add to the hot oil, cooking for 1 to 2 minutes, until golden brown on each side. Using tongs, transfer the cooked onion rings to paper towels to drain and then repeat with the remaining onion rings until all are cooked. Place the onion rings on a platter and serve with the dipping sauce.

## orange marmalade dipping sauce (makes 1 cup)

½ cup orange marmalade
¼ cup Dijon mustard

¼ cup honey

In a small bowl, whisk together the orange marmalade, Dijon mustard, and honey.

# grilled antipasto platter

## makes 6 to 8 servings

This grilled vegetable salad is a common dish in Europe but definitely does not get the attention it deserves here in the States. It is the perfect platter to make as an appetizer or a vegetarian entrée. You can also turn it into a full meal for nonvegetarians by adding deli meats or prosciutto.

1 cup extra-virgin olive oil, plus extra for drizzling
4 cloves garlic, minced
3 sprigs fresh rosemary, chopped
Kosher salt and freshly ground black pepper
¼ cup sun-dried tomatoes
2 zucchini, cut lengthwise into ½-inch slices
2 yellow squash, cut lengthwise into ½-inch slices
1 medium eggplant, cut into ½-inch slices
2 large portobello mushrooms, stems removed

2 medium red onions, cut into ½-inch slices
12 asparagus spears, tough ends trimmed
3 Italian frying peppers
1 bulb fennel, cut into quarters
1 lemon, sliced ½ inch thick
1 (6-ounce) jar marinated artichokes, drained
1 cup kalamata olives
6 fresh basil leaves, slivered
White balsamic vinegar, for drizzling

Preheat a grill to medium heat.

In a small saucepan over low heat, whisk together the oil, garlic, rosemary, and salt and pepper to taste. Heat for 5 minutes and then set aside to cool. Cover the sun-dried tomatoes with hot water for 10 minutes and drain.

Brush the grill grates with oil. Brush the zucchini, yellow squash, eggplant, mushrooms, red onions, asparagus, frying peppers, fennel, and lemon slices with the herbed garlic oil. Place the vegetables on the preheated grill and cook for 4 to 5 minutes per side, until slightly charred on the edges and tender. Remove the peppers from the grill, remove the stems and seeds, and then cut into strips.

Arrange the grilled vegetables on a platter along with the sun-dried tomatoes, artichokes, and olives. Sprinkle with basil and season with salt and pepper to taste. Garnish with the grilled lemon slices and drizzle with extra-virgin olive oil and white balsamic vinegar.

# tangy peanut butter chicken skewers

## makes 4 to 6 servings

Peanut butter is most often expected to appear with bread and jelly, with chocolate, or in cookies. This appetizer, combining creamy peanut butter, spices, brown sugar, and chicken, is fun and tasty for everyone. My five-year-old eats these skewers like lollipops.

2 pounds boneless, skinless chicken breasts, cut into 1-inch strips
Wooden skewers, soaked in water for 20 minutes
Salt and freshly ground black pepper
½ cup creamy peanut butter
¼ cup gluten-free chicken broth
¼ cup water

¼ cup gluten-free soy sauce
2 garlic cloves, minced
2 tablespoons freshly squeezed lime juice
2 tablespoons brown sugar
½ teaspoon ground ginger
⅛ teaspoon cayenne
1 tablespoon chopped fresh cilantro

Preheat a grill to medium-high heat.

Weave the chicken onto the skewers and place on a plate. Sprinkle with salt and pepper and set aside.

In a medium saucepan over medium-high heat, combine the peanut butter, chicken broth, water, soy sauce, garlic, lime juice, brown sugar, ginger, and cayenne. Cook, stirring, until smooth and hot; set aside.

Place the chicken skewers on the preheated grill and brush generously with the peanut butter sauce. Cook for about 3 minutes, until nicely browned, then turn and brush with sauce on the other side. Continue to cook, brushing on more sauces until the chicken is cooked through, 3 to 4 minutes. Place the chicken skewers on a serving platter and sprinkle with cilantro.

# arancini (rice balls with cheese)

## makes 2 dozen

These are an Italian treat—risotto balls stuffed with your favorite cheese, breaded, and deep-fried. They are fabulous! Be forewarned that you won't stop at just one.

2 cups gluten-free chicken broth
1 cup Arborio rice
½ cup finely grated Parmesan cheese
2 tablespoons chopped fresh parsley
½ teaspoon garlic powder
¼ teaspoon freshly ground black pepper

2 eggs, separated
½ cup gluten-free bread crumbs
About 2 ounces cheese (such as mozzarella, sharp provolone, or Monterey Jack), cut into 24 (½-inch) cubes
Vegetable oil, for deep frying

Place the chicken broth in a medium saucepan over high heat and bring to a boil. Stir in the rice, cover the pan, lower the heat, and simmer for 20 to 25 minutes, until all the water is absorbed.

Transfer the rice to a large bowl and stir in the Parmesan cheese, parsley, garlic powder, and pepper. Allow the rice to cool slightly and then stir in the egg yolks.

In a separate shallow bowl, beat the egg whites until frothy.

Place the bread crumbs in a third bowl.

Take 1 tablespoon of the rice mixture in the palm of your hand, place a cube of cheese in the middle, and form a ball around the cheese. Continue until all the rice balls are made, occasionally rinsing your hands to keep the rice from sticking to your hands. Roll the rice balls in the egg whites and then in the bread crumbs, placing them on a platter as you bread them.

In a large saucepan, heat 3 inches of vegetable oil until a deep-fat thermometer reads 360°F. Carefully lower 6 to 8 rice balls at a time into the hot oil and cook until dark golden brown, 1 to 2 minutes. Remove with tongs or a slotted spoon and drain on paper towels. The rice balls can be kept warm in a low oven until ready to serve.

# spinach parmesan bites with honey mustard dipping sauce

## makes 3 dozen

The savory stuffing mix by Aleia's holds these spinach, onion, and Parmesan cheese bites together perfectly. Its unique flavor combines with the honey mustard dipping sauce to leave guests wanting more and more.

¼ cup Dijon mustard
¼ cup honey
2 (10-ounce) packages frozen chopped spinach, thawed and squeezed dry
2 cups Aleia's Savory Stuffing mix, finely ground

1 cup finely grated Parmesan cheese
8 tablespoons (1 stick) unsalted butter, melted
4 green onions, finely chopped
3 eggs, beaten
¼ teaspoon garlic powder

In a small bowl, whisk together the Dijon mustard and honey. Set aside until needed.

In a large bowl, mix together the spinach, stuffing mix, Parmesan cheese, melted butter, green onions, eggs, and garlic powder. Using your hands, shape the mixture into 1-inch balls, place on a platter, cover with plastic wrap, and refrigerate overnight.

Preheat the oven to 350°F. Grease a baking sheet.

Place the spinach bites on the prepared pan and bake for 15 to 20 minutes, until golden brown. Serve with the honey mustard sauce.

# sharp cheddar potato croquettes

## makes 1 dozen

These sharp cheddar cheese and potato croquettes are slightly crunchy on the outside and creamy in the middle—a cross between mashed potato and cheese fries.

1 cup water
⅓ cup plus 1 teaspoon milk
1 cup Betty Crocker Potato Buds
¼ cup plus 1 tablespoon finely grated Parmesan cheese
¼ teaspoon kosher salt
⅛ teaspoon freshly ground black pepper

2 ounces sharp cheddar cheese, cut into ½-inch cubes
¼ cup white rice flour
1 egg
¼ cup gluten-free bread crumbs
Vegetable oil, for deep frying

In a medium saucepan, bring the water and ⅓ cup of the milk to a boil.

Remove the pan from the heat and stir in the instant mashed potatoes. Allow the potatoes to rest for 5 minutes (the potatoes will be stiff).

Stir in ¼ cup of the Parmesan cheese, the salt, and the pepper.

Cover the potato dough with plastic wrap and refrigerate until cold.

Using a tablespoon, scoop the potatoes and roll between your palms to form 1½-inch balls. Push a cheddar cube into the center of each potato ball and roll again to seal.

Place the flour in a shallow bowl. In a separate bowl, beat together the egg and the remaining teaspoon of milk.

Combine the bread crumbs and the remaining tablespoon of Parmesan cheese in a shallow dish.

Roll the potato balls in the flour, dip in the egg mixture, and then dredge in the bread crumbs.

Fill a saucepan halfway with vegetable oil and heat over medium-high heat until a deep-fat thermometer reads 360°F.

Fry the potato croquettes for 2 to 3 minutes, until golden brown. Drain on paper towels and serve warm.

# cheesy crab, spinach, and artichoke dip

makes 8 to 10 servings

baking time: 30 minutes

Chock-full of spinach and artichoke, with nearly as much vegetable as cheese, this dip is a rare find. The sour cream, crabmeat, and cheese blend makes it a salty, chunky, and incredibly delicious warm dip, perfect on tortilla or corn chips or for dipping carrot or celery sticks.

1 (14-ounce) can artichoke hearts, drained and quartered
1 (10-ounce) package frozen spinach, thawed and squeezed dry
1 (8-ounce) can crabmeat
1 (8-ounce) package cream cheese, at room temperature
½ cup mayonnaise
¼ cup sour cream
½ cup shredded cheddar cheese
½ cup shredded Monterey Jack cheese
½ cup plus 2 tablespoons finely grated Parmesan cheese
1 tablespoon Creole or stone-ground mustard
1 teaspoon gluten-free Worcestershire sauce
½ teaspoon kosher salt
½ teaspoon onion powder
¼ teaspoon cayenne
1 egg yolk
Tortilla chips, for serving

Preheat the oven to 350°F and grease an 11 by 7-inch casserole dish.

Using an electric mixer with the paddle attachment or a hand mixer, beat together the artichoke hearts, spinach, crab, cream cheese, mayonnaise, sour cream, cheddar, Monterey Jack, ½ cup of the Parmesan, the mustard, Worcestershire sauce, kosher salt, onion powder, cayenne, and egg yolk.

Pour the crab mixture into the prepared casserole dish, sprinkle evenly with the remaining 2 tablespoons Parmesan cheese, and bake until the top is golden brown and the center is hot, 30 minutes. Serve warm with tortilla chips.

# savor your salad

With so many flavors, consistencies, and varieties available, buying salad dressing at the local grocery store, in lieu of making one from scratch, has become the norm. Most people don't give it a second thought. However, for those with celiac disease it is a challenge to stand in that aisle and carefully read every ingredient and additive to ensure that a dressing is completely wheat and gluten free. I have been surprised over the years at how many times the sales personnel of major food distributors have sent dressing samples to me at work, assuring me that they are gluten free, when they actually contain malt vinegar or a wheat derivative. This is just one advantage of opting for a delicious homemade dressing. While it might take a few minutes to mix, it provides a great degree of assurance that no unexpected digestive difficulties will result from enjoying a bowl of greens. It can also help you discover fresh new flavors that will make your taste buds dance, as well as "real" consistencies that aren't hampered by artificial gums and gooey textures.

I humbly admit that my wife is more of a salad fan than I am. She is happy with a big bowl of crisp greens, teeming with raw vegetables and enhanced with cheese or nuts and a really nice dressing. This is perhaps what most people envision when they think of a salad. When I think of a salad, I picture a hearty Roasted Beet Salad with Goat Cheese and Candied Walnuts, or perhaps a Chicken and Cucumber Sesame Noodle Salad, or even The Perfect Caesar Salad with Herbed Croutons. These can satisfy even the pickiest of salad eaters while providing powerful flavors and a good deal of nutrition.

When I do prepare a traditional salad with greens and vegetables, there is a set of simple rules I follow to ensure that it will be of the highest quality and never pushed to the side when served at our table. One easy measure is to make sure that the greens are cleaned thoroughly with cold water (never with soap) and then placed in a salad spinner to remove all the excess water. The old adage "oil and water don't mix" has particular relevance here. When salad dressing is poured over wet greens, the dressing just slides off, leaving the greens soggy, mushy, and quite unappetizing. When I was in high school, I pulled into the driveway one day to find my stepmother, who was born and raised in France, standing in the front yard, spinning a clean pillowcase in circles over her head. I confirmed that she was indeed sober, and she explained that her salad spinner had broken and that she needed to dry the greens before making her salad for the company that was on the way. And, yes, the pillowcase really did work.

A second rule: Before assembling the salad, make sure the greens are cold, crisp, and crunchy. I usually place my washed and dried greens in a glass bowl, cover them with a clean dish towel, and place them in the back of the refrigerator, where the temperature is coldest.

Be prudent with the amount of dressing you add to the greens. A salad should not look as if one could drink it. The greens and vegetables should carry just enough dressing to complement their flavors, not overpower them.

Finally, remember that making a salad should be a fun and creative endeavor. Think outside the box, or at least outside the bottle. On page 42 you will find a salad cheat sheet I designed to help you create salads that go beyond mere lettuce and tomatoes. I hope you will enjoy preparing and devouring them at least as much as my wife does!

The following chart is just a sample of some of the tasty ingredients you can use to jazz up the average salad. Try combining some of your favorite ingredients into your own unique and delicious salad and then topping it with one of the homemade dressings in this chapter.

| lettuce greens | |
|---|---|
| | **Iceberg:** Very popular because it maintains its crispiness for a relatively long time, has very mild flavor and very nearly zero calories. |
| | **Romaine:** Crispy, mild-flavored leaves with a crunchy texture that works very well with most dressings. It's the lettuce of choice in a classic Caesar salad. |
| | **Butter, Boston, or Bibb:** Softer lettuce with a tender texture and mild flavor. |
| | **Red tip leaf or green leaf lettuce:** Both have a mild and delicate flavor, can be bought in huge bunches, and have staying power in the crisper. |
| | **Spinach:** A dark, leafy green with a unique flavor and delicate texture. Very nutrient dense, chock-full of vitamins, minerals, and fiber. |
| | **Arugula:** A peppery lettuce that works well mixed with milder greens—a great way to kick the flavor up a notch in an average salad. |
| | **Radicchio:** A bitter and peppery-flavored green. Small amounts blended with milder lettuces work best. |
| | **Curly endive:** A crunchy and slightly bitter green that needs to be blended with milder greens. |
| | **Mesclun:** A catchall term usually referring to a blend of younger greens, some with spicy flavors. Might include varieties such as arugula, watercress, mizuna, mustard greens, and sorrel. |

| vegetables | Tomatoes | Green beans | Hot peppers: |
| | Celery | Snap peas | jalapeños or |
| | Onions: red, yellow, | Broccoli | serranos |
| | white | Cauliflower | Cucumbers |
| | Green onions | Peas | Asparagus |
| | Carrots | Artichokes | Squash |
| | Radishes | Bell peppers: red, | Beets |
| | Zucchini | yellow, green | Mushrooms |
| | | | Jícama |

| fruit | Strawberries | Raspberries | Dried cranberries |
| | Peaches | Blackberries | Dried cherries |
| | Avocados | Pineapple | Dried apricots |
| | Plums | Grapes | Olives |
| | Blueberries | Oranges | |
| | Apples | Raisins | |

| nuts/seeds/beans | Almonds | Peanuts | Poppy seeds |
| | Walnuts | Cashews | Sunflower seeds |
| | Hazelnuts | Pine nuts | Beans (any) |
| | Pecans | Pumpkin seeds | Shredded coconut |
| | Pistachios | Sesame seeds | |

| fresh herbs | Parsley | Dill | Oregano |
| | Cilantro | Mint | Thyme |

| proteins | Hard-boiled eggs | Tuna | Tofu |
| | Crispy bacon | Chicken | |
| | Cold cuts: turkey, | Salmon | |
| | ham, roast beef, | Shrimp | |
| | salami, and others | Lean Beef | |

| shredded, crumbled, or cubed cheese | Mozzarella | Provolone | Monterey Jack |
| | Feta/goat | American | Pepper Jack |
| | Parmesan | Blue | Asiago |
| | Swiss | Cheddar | |

# honey balsamic vinaigrette

## makes about ¾ cup

A light and snappy dressing that adds sweetness and pizzazz to any bowl of lettuce, this has become a favorite summer salad dressing at our barbecues and dinner parties.

¼ cup balsamic vinegar
1 tablespoon plus 1 teaspoon Dijon mustard
1 tablespoon honey

¼ teaspoon salt
¼ teaspoon freshly ground black pepper
½ cup extra-virgin olive oil

In a large bowl, whisk together the vinegar, mustard, honey, salt, and pepper.

Slowly drizzle in the oil, whisking constantly, until the dressing is emulsified.

Store in an airtight container in the refrigerator.

variations: Add 1 clove garlic, minced, or ¼ teaspoon garlic powder.

Add 1 teaspoon dried oregano or Italian seasoning.

# buttermilk ranch dressing

## makes 1 cup

Once you try the fresh, clean taste of homemade salad dressings, you'll never want a store-bought bottle again. The buttermilk, mayonnaise, and sour cream churned with onions, lemon juice, and multiple spices make an exciting dish out of your plain old greens.

¼ cup buttermilk
¼ cup mayonnaise
¼ cup sour cream
2 teaspoons minced yellow onion
½ teaspoon freshly squeezed lemon juice
¼ teaspoon dry mustard
¼ teaspoon garlic powder

1 tablespoon finely chopped fresh parsley
½ teaspoon finely chopped fresh chives
¼ teaspoon dried dill or ¾ teaspoon chopped fresh
¼ teaspoon salt
⅛ teaspoon freshly ground black pepper
Pinch of cayenne (optional)

In a medium bowl, whisk together all the ingredients. Refrigerate for up to 1 week.

# hearty blue cheese dressing

## makes 1½ cups

If you have never tasted a homemade blue cheese dressing, it is time to give it a try. This creamy dressing with giant chunks of tangy blue cheese is fantastic on crisp salad greens. And at your next Super Bowl party, slather it all over your buffalo chicken wings.

½ cup sour cream
½ cup mayonnaise
¼ pound blue cheese, crumbled
2 tablespoons buttermilk

1½ teaspoons freshly squeezed lemon juice
2 tablespoons finely chopped green onion
¼ teaspoon salt
⅛ teaspoon freshly ground black pepper

In a medium bowl, whisk together all the ingredients. Place in a sealed container and refrigerate for up to 1 week.

chef's note: Some blue cheese producers still use wheat-based breads as starters for the production of cheese. So it is very important that you read the labels on the package.

# french dressing

## makes about 1 cup

No more chemicals or stabilizers to gum up your salad dressing or soak out the health benefits of your veggies and greens. This light and delicious adaptation of the popular French dressing is altogether low-fat, spicy, garlicky, and sweet!

½ cup extra-virgin olive oil
¼ cup apple cider vinegar
6 tablespoons granulated sugar
1 teaspoon paprika
1 teaspoon gluten-free Worcestershire sauce

1 teaspoon garlic powder
⅛ teaspoon freshly ground black pepper
2 teaspoons Dijon mustard
1 tablespoon minced onion

In a medium bowl, whisk together the olive oil, vinegar, sugar, paprika, Worcestershire sauce, garlic powder, and black pepper.

Place the Dijon mustard in a separate bowl, and whisk constantly while slowly adding the oil mixture, until the dressing is emulsified. Stir in the onion and store in an airtight container in the refrigerator for up to 1 week.

# garlicky caesar dressing

## makes 1 cup

Use this smooth and creamy classic and some Herbed Croutons (recipe follows) on The Perfect Caesar Salad on page 49.

3 cloves garlic, peeled
¾ cup mayonnaise
2 tablespoons finely grated Parmesan cheese
1 tablespoon freshly squeezed lemon juice

1 teaspoon gluten-free Worcestershire sauce
1 teaspoon Dijon mustard
½ teaspoon anchovy paste
1 tablespoon extra-virgin olive oil

Place the garlic in a food processor and process to chop. Add the mayonnaise, Parmesan cheese, lemon juice, Worcestershire sauce, mustard, and anchovy paste. Process until blended, then drizzle in the olive oil with the food processor running until the dressing is emulsified. Refrigerate in an airtight container for up to 1 week.

# herbed croutons

## makes 5 cups

No salad is complete without crunchy, buttery croutons. These croutons are the perfect finishing touch for a Caesar salad or your favorite tossed salad.

1 (12-ounce) loaf Udi's Whole Grain Bread, cut into 1-inch cubes
4 tablespoons (½ stick) unsalted butter, melted
2 tablespoons olive oil

1 teaspoon dried oregano
1 teaspoon garlic powder
½ teaspoon kosher salt
⅛ teaspoon cayenne

Preheat the oven to 350°F and place the cubed bread in a large bowl.

In a small bowl, whisk together the melted butter, olive oil, oregano, garlic powder, salt, and cayenne. Drizzle the mixture over the cubed bread and toss gently to coat.

Pour the cubes onto a sheet pan in a single layer and bake for 25 to 30 minutes, turning occasionally, until golden brown. Allow to cool on the pan and then store in an airtight container for up to 1 week.

# the perfect caesar salad
# with herbed croutons

makes 4 servings

A garlicky Caesar topped with big crunchy croutons is a favorite salad choice for so many. This tangy and sumptuous version can make for a full and healthy meal when topped with grilled or blackened chicken, shrimp, or salmon.

1 pound romaine lettuce, chopped
¼ cup Garlicky Caesar Dressing (page 48)
¼ cup finely grated Parmesan cheese

1 cup Herbed Croutons (page 48)
Salt and freshly ground black pepper

Place the chopped romaine in a large bowl and toss with the dressing.

Add the Parmesan cheese and croutons and toss to blend. Season to taste with salt and pepper.

# fried green tomato salad with garlicky herb cheese and white beans

## makes 6 servings

What do you do when your sons wander into the garden and pick all the not-yet-ripe tomatoes? You create a new salad with fried green tomatoes, garlicky herb cheese, and a simple can of white beans. This salad turns a classic southern staple into a posh restaurant specialty

2 tablespoons extra-virgin olive oil
2 tablespoons white balsamic vinegar
1 tablespoon honey
¼ teaspoon Dijon mustard
1 teaspoon finely chopped fresh parsley
1 clove garlic, minced
½ teaspoon plus ⅛ teaspoon salt
1 (15-ounce) can white beans, drained, rinsed, and dried
¼ cup finely diced red bell pepper

1 cup yellow cornmeal
2 teaspoons garlic powder
¼ teaspoon freshly ground black pepper
1 egg
1 tablespoon buttermilk
4 green tomatoes, cored and sliced ¼ inch thick (24 slices)
Vegetable oil, for frying
6 tablespoons Garlicky Herbed Cheese Spread (page 29)

In a medium bowl, whisk together the olive oil, vinegar, honey, mustard, parsley, garlic, and ⅛ teaspoon of the salt. Add the beans and red pepper, tossing to coat thoroughly in the dressing. Set aside.

In a shallow small bowl, whisk together the cornmeal, garlic powder, the remaining ½ teaspoon of salt, and the pepper. In another shallow bowl, beat together the egg and buttermilk.

Heat ¼ inch vegetable oil in a large sauté pan or skillet over medium-high heat. Dip each tomato slice in the egg mixture, allow the excess to drip off, and dredge both sides in the cornmeal.

Fry in the hot oil until golden brown on both sides, 3 to 4 minutes per side, and then place on paper towels to drain. Continue until all the tomato slices are fried.

To build each salad, place a fried tomato on a serving plate, followed by a teaspoon of cheese. Layer on 3 more tomato slices with 2 more teaspoons of cheese, ending with a tomato slice. Using a spoon, scoop the bean dressing over the top of the salad and around the bottom of the tomatoes. Serve immediately.

# walnut and four-bean salad

## makes 8 to 10 servings

This very filling and nutritious four-bean salad gets a unique twist with walnut vinaigrette dressing. The toasted walnut oil is a delicious alternative to olive oil, and it adds a rich, nutty flavor to this and other homemade salad dressings.

½ pound green beans, cut in half
½ cup diced celery
½ cup diced red onion
1 (15-ounce) can red kidney beans, rinsed, drained, and dried
1 (15-ounce) can garbanzo beans (chickpeas), drained, rinsed, and dried
1 (15-ounce) can navy beans, rinsed, drained, and dried

⅓ cup toasted walnut oil
⅓ cup red wine vinegar
¼ cup granulated sugar
1 clove garlic, minced
1 tablespoon finely chopped fresh parsley
¾ teaspoon salt
¼ teaspoon freshly ground black pepper

Bring a large pot of salted water to a boil over high heat. Add the green beans and cook for 3 to 4 minutes, until tender. Drain and place the beans in a bowl of ice water to cool. Remove from the water and place on a baking sheet covered with a clean dish towel to dry.

In a large mixing bowl, combine the celery, red onion, kidney beans, garbanzo beans, navy beans, and green beans.

In a medium bowl, whisk together the walnut oil, vinegar, sugar, garlic, parsley, salt, and pepper. Add the dressing to the beans and toss until thoroughly mixed and coated with the dressing. Refrigerate overnight before serving.

# roasted beet salad with goat cheese and candied walnuts

## makes 4 to 6 servings

## cooking time: 1½ hours

This is the salad to beat all salads, with sweet and buttery roasted beets chopped into tiny cubes and covered in salty goat cheese and sugared walnuts—simply spectacular!

1½ pound beets, trimmed and washed
½ cup walnut halves
¼ cup plus ½ teaspoon granulated sugar
Pinch of cayenne
1½ teaspoons white balsamic vinegar
1 tablespoon Dijon mustard
1 tablespoon honey
¼ cup plus 1 tablespoon extra-virgin
   olive oil

¼ teaspoon Kosher salt
⅛ teaspoon freshly ground black pepper
1 medium yellow onion, caramelized
   (page 182)
¼ pound goat cheese, crumbled
Baby arugula or baby spinach, slivered, for
   garnish

Preheat the oven to 350°F.

Wrap each beet in aluminum foil and bake for 1½ hours, or until a skewer inserted through the foil into the beet slides in easily.

While the beets are cooking, place the walnuts, sugar, and cayenne in a medium sauté pan over medium heat. Stir the nuts until the sugar dissolves into a liquid and coats the nuts, 5 to 6 minutes. Pour the walnuts out of the skillet onto a piece of foil to cool.

Remove the beets from the oven and allow to cool for 30 to 40 minutes. To peel the beets, place them under cold running water and, using your fingers, remove the skins.

Dice the beets and place in a large mixing bowl.

In a small bowl, whisk together the vinegar, mustard, and honey. Gradually whisk in the oil, salt, and pepper until the dressing is emulsified.

Pour the dressing over the beets and toss until thoroughly coated. Sprinkle the beets with the caramelized onion, candied walnuts, and goat cheese. Top with a nest of arugula just before serving.

# bacon, lettuce, and tomato wedge salad

## makes 4 servings

This is the salad version of a most popular sandwich, and it's so simple to assemble you won't believe how good it really is. A thick dressing gives it weight and substance.

1 head iceberg lettuce, quartered
1 cup Hearty Blue Cheese Dressing (page 46)
   or Buttermilk Ranch Dressing (page 45)
1 cup diced tomato

¼ cup diced green onion
½ cup crumbled crisp-cooked bacon
   (from about 8 strips)

Pick up the head of lettuce with both hands and strike the core on a cutting board to loosen and remove. Cut the head in half and then in half again to produce 4 wedges. Place the wedges on individual plates and drizzle each with ¼ cup of the dressing. Sprinkle each wedge with ¼ cup tomato, 1 tablespoon green onion, and 2 tablespoons bacon crumbles. Serve immediately.

# cherry walnut quinoa salad

## makes 4 to 6 servings

With its increasing popularity and notoriety for its health benefits, people are experimenting with different ways to serve quinoa. Quinoa is a gluten-free grain packed with 8 grams of protein, 5 grams of fiber, and only 220 calories per cup. Making a cold quinoa salad is a unique and fun way to start off a meal. This one also combines broccoli, cranberries or dried cherries, red onion, and walnuts for a unique flavor and texture experience.

1 cup quinoa
2 cups water
1½ cups chopped broccoli florets
1 cup dried cherries or cranberries
¼ cup finely chopped red onion
¼ cup chopped walnuts

¼ cup white balsamic vinegar
2 tablespoons extra-virgin olive oil
3 cloves garlic, minced
½ teaspoon salt
¼ teaspoon freshly ground black pepper

In a medium saucepan, bring the quinoa and water to a boil over high heat.

Lower the heat to simmer, cover, and cook until all the water is absorbed, 10 to 15 minutes.

Scoop the cooked quinoa onto a large plate and allow to cool completely.

In a medium bowl, mix together the broccoli, dried cherries, red onion, walnuts, and cooked quinoa.

In a small bowl, whisk together the vinegar, olive oil, garlic, salt, and pepper.

Add to the quinoa mixture and toss until completely blended. Refrigerate overnight to allow the flavors to meld.

# fattoush

## makes 4 to 6 servings

My coworker, Chef Lisa, first introduced me to this Lebanese salad, which is usually made with toasted pita bread and seasonal vegetables and herbs. I loved it so much that I immediately began working on a gluten-free version. Food for Life Brown Rice Tortillas make the perfect pita substitute so that now all can enjoy it.

2 brown rice tortillas, each cut into 8 wedges
¼ cup olive oil plus 2 tablespoons olive oil
1 teaspoon ground sumac
2 cups cubed tomatoes
1 cup drained canned artichoke hearts
½ cup cubed cucumber
½ cup diced red bell pepper
½ cup diced red onion

½ cup sliced radishes
2 tablespoons finely chopped fresh parsley
2 tablespoons finely chopped fresh mint
1 cup crumbled feta cheese
¼ cup kalamata olives, pitted and halved
¼ cup freshly squeezed lemon juice
2 cloves garlic, minced
Salt and freshly ground black pepper

Preheat the oven to 350°F.

Place the tortilla wedges in a bowl and toss with 2 tablespoons of the olive oil and the sumac. Place in a single layer on a baking sheet and bake until crispy, 10 to 12 minutes. Set aside.

In a large bowl, toss together the tomatoes, artichoke hearts, cucumber, red pepper, onion, radishes, parsley, mint, feta, and olives.

In a small bowl, whisk together the remaining ¼ cup olive oil, the lemon juice, and the garlic. Pour over the salad and toss to coat. Season the salad with salt and pepper to taste and then mix in the crispy tortillas just before serving.

chef's note: Sumac is a Middle Eastern spice that has a tart, fruity flavor. It can be found at most supermarkets.

# roasted corn, tomato, and avocado salad

## makes 4 to 6 servings

We love this salad next to a nice hunk of salmon and a big piece of gluten-free crusty bread. It is colorful, sumptuous, healthy, and light.

3 cups corn kernels
1 tablespoon olive oil
½ teaspoon kosher salt, plus extra for
   sprinkling
2 cups diced seeded cucumber
1½ cups grape tomatoes, halved
¼ cup finely diced red onion

2 green onions, finely chopped
1 jalapeño pepper, seeded and minced
½ teaspoon ground cumin
¼ cup freshly squeezed lime juice
¼ cup chopped fresh cilantro
2 avocados, peeled, pitted, and chopped

Preheat the oven to 400°F.

Place the corn on a baking sheet, drizzle with the olive oil, and sprinkle with salt.

Roast for 15 to 20 minutes, until the edges of the corn begin to brown. Remove from the oven and set aside to cool.

In a large bowl, toss together the cucumber, tomatoes, red onion, green onions, jalapeño, cumin, lime juice, cilantro, and corn. Stir in the avocados and remaining ½ teaspoon salt and refrigerate until ready to serve.

# panzanella

## makes 4 servings

A rustic Italian salad is a delicious way to use up that day-old gluten-free bread. Vine-ripened tomatoes, hand-picked basil, fresh mozzarella, and kalamata olives tossed with extra-virgin olive oil and red wine vinegar make a colorful and delicious start to a meal.

2 cups crusty gluten-free bread, cut into
   1-inch cubes
¼ cup extra-virgin olive oil
2 tablespoons red wine vinegar
2 cloves garlic, minced
¼ teaspoon salt

⅛ teaspoon freshly ground black pepper
1 pound tomatoes, cored and cut into bite-
   sized chunks
½ cup small fresh mozzarella balls, halved
¼ cup kalamata olives, pitted and halved
¼ cup coarsely chopped fresh basil leaves

Preheat the oven to 400°F. Spread the bread cubes evenly on a baking sheet and cook until toasted and golden brown, 8 to 10 minutes. Allow the bread to cool slightly.

Meanwhile, in a small bowl, whisk together the olive oil, vinegar, garlic, salt, and pepper. Set aside.

In a large bowl, combine the tomatoes, mozzarella, olives, basil, and bread cubes. Add the dressing and toss until thoroughly coated. Allow the salad to rest for 5 to 10 minutes before serving.

# blue cheese and pear coleslaw

## makes 12 servings

The salty blue cheese and sugary pear combination makes for an elegant salad or side dish. I took this to a baptism at our parish. Ever since, it has been requested for countless potluck events.

½ cup sugar
½ cup sour cream
½ cup buttermilk
½ cup mayonnaise
¼ cup freshly squeezed lemon juice
2 tablespoons plus 2 teaspoons white
   vinegar

2 pounds coleslaw mix
¼ cup shredded carrot
3 Bosc pears, peeled, cored, and diced
½ pound blue cheese
Salt and freshly ground black pepper

In a medium bowl, whisk together the sugar, sour cream, buttermilk, mayonnaise, lemon juice, and vinegar. Set aside.

In a large bowl, combine the coleslaw mix, carrot, and pears. Add the dressing and toss until thoroughly incorporated. Crumble in the blue cheese and toss until blended. Add salt and pepper to taste. Refrigerate overnight; then mix again just before serving.

chef's note: Can be made 1 day ahead.

# chicken and cucumber sesame noodle salad

## makes 4 to 6 servings

We call this pasta dish a salad, but it can also stand on its own when you need a quick meal. It combines chicken and rice noodles with crisp vegetables, Asian sauces, and the crunch of sesame seeds and peanuts. Serve it warm, or transfer it cold from the fridge to the picnic basket. Notta pasta works extremely well with this dish.

½ pound rice spaghetti or rice stick noodles
1 pound boneless, skinless chicken breast,
   cut into ½-inch pieces
Salt and freshly ground black pepper
2 teaspoons olive oil
¼ cup rice vinegar
2 tablespoons toasted sesame oil
2 tablespoons gluten-free soy sauce
2 teaspoons sweet chili sauce
1 tablespoon honey

2 cloves garlic, minced
½ teaspoon finely minced fresh ginger
2 medium cucumbers, halved lengthwise
   and sliced (about 3 cups)
½ cup shredded carrot
½ cup chopped green onion
¼ cup finely chopped unsalted dry-roasted
   peanuts
½ teaspoon black sesame seeds
6 lime wedges, for serving (optional)

Cook the rice spaghetti according to the package directions. Drain, rinse under cold water, and set aside.

Meanwhile, season the chicken with salt and pepper. In a medium sauté pan, heat the olive oil over medium-high heat and cook the chicken for about 4 minutes, stirring, until cooked through. Set aside to cool.

In a large bowl, whisk together the vinegar, sesame oil, soy sauce, chili sauce, honey, garlic, and ginger. Add the noodles, cucumbers, carrot, green onion, chicken, and peanuts, tossing until mixed.

Sprinkle with the sesame seeds and serve with lime wedges to squeeze on top.

# tasty comforts

When Angela and I first met, we both worked as banquet managers at a local country club, known for the catered delights served at its golf outings, showers, and elaborate weddings. The main building had a beautiful ballroom constructed of floor-to-ceiling windows, displaying a spectacular look at the beautiful eastern Connecticut landscape. During the heart of wedding season we often ran six to eight receptions a weekend and began to look upon the club as our "home away from home" because of the countless hours we spent there, both day and night.

During one particularly crazy season, all five of Angela's siblings worked alongside us, as waiters, bus boys, bartenders, and other staff. Michael, Eddie, Kevin, Kathleen, and Maryanna all worked hard, endured long shifts, and helped us pull off some unbelievable events. One of the motivators for remaining on their feet and running in all directions for many hours was knowing that a free meal was waiting for everyone at the end of the night. After the wedding guests were taken care of, all of our staff would sit down and enjoy the same meal as the guests. One favorite entrée was the Golden Walnut Baked Stuffed Shrimp, made with a buttery cracker crumb filling and stuffed with lump crabmeat, ground walnuts, and a drizzle of white wine. This wasn't a run-of-the-mill entrée but one of those "Wow!" dishes that gets seared into your memory.

Years later, when we all had matured (or at the very least gotten older) Angela and I began hosting Christmas Eve dinner at our home. Maryanna called and requested that I make the stuffed shrimp—the one she continued to dream about. Changing that dish into its perfect, gluten-free counterpart was a real challenge. But after making it work, I went on a mission to conquer some of the most memorable dishes I had savored during my years in the restaurant business. Some are naturally gluten free, but most are not and needed painstaking measurement and lots of trial and error to get them just right, such as the Creole Sausage and Shrimp with Creamy Grits and the Buttery Herb-Crumbed Scallops and Mushrooms. I also developed Plum Barbecued Baby Back Ribs for hot summer days.

Favorite comfort foods are often unique to an individual and are influenced by where one lives, what foods were traditional on Thanksgiving or Easter, or what Mom put on the table on cold winter nights. The Southern-Style Chicken and Dumplings were created to answer an e-mail request from Beth who had missed the dish so much since embracing her gluten-free lifestyle. I dedicate the Italian Herb-Crusted Salmon and Pretzel-Crusted Tilapia with Dijon Cream Sauce to Diane at the Frog Bridge Gymnastic Studio, who asked earnestly for more fish, more fish, and more fish. The Pistachio-and-Mustard-Encrusted Lamb Chops are for Roy and Robin Kerlin and his family, who love lamb so much they started their own sheep farm called Morning Star Meadows Farm in North Stonington, Connecticut. I hope that each of the dishes in this chapter affords you some much-sought-after gastronomic delight and some well-deserved good memories and comfort on all of your sunny days, holidays, and chilly nights.

# southern-style chicken and dumplings

## makes 4 to 6 servings

This recipe is the culmination of a desperate e-mail request from a young woman from the South: How can we make a delicious and satisfying chicken and dumpling soup like the one Gramma used to make for the holidays? This gluten-free version is a true southern comfort!

### Dumplings

1 cup white rice flour
1 teaspoon baking powder
¼ teaspoon salt
1 tablespoon butter, cubed, plus 1
    tablespoon butter, melted
½ cup milk
1 egg
1 tablespoon finely chopped fresh parsley

### Chicken and Vegetables

1 tablespoon olive oil
2 tablespoons butter

1½ cups chopped yellow onions
1 cup diced carrots
½ cup diced celery
1 bay leaf
1 teaspoon dried thyme leaves
1 tablespoon dry sherry
1 teaspoon poultry seasoning
1 tablespoon white rice flour
1½ quarts gluten-free chicken broth
1 tablespoon half-and-half
1½ pounds shredded cooked chicken
Salt and freshly ground black pepper
1 cup frozen peas, thawed

To make the dumplings: In a large bowl, whisk together the white rice flour, baking powder, and salt. Add the cubed butter and, using your hands, rub the butter and flour between your fingertips until blended. Add the melted butter, milk, egg, and parsley and, using a fork, mix thoroughly until a batter forms. Set aside.

To make the chicken and vegetables: Heat the olive oil and butter in a large pot over medium-high heat. Add the onions, carrots, celery, bay leaf, and thyme and cook, stirring frequently, for 2 minutes. Add the sherry, cook for 1 minute, and then stir in the poultry seasoning and white rice flour. Cook for 1 more minute, then add the chicken broth, half-and-half, and cooked chicken. Bring to a boil and season to taste with salt and pepper. Drop spoonfuls of dumpling batter on top of the simmering stew, cover the pot with a tight-fitting lid, reduce the heat to medium-low, and steam the dumplings until cooked, about 10 minutes. Gently stir in the peas, then cook for a minute or two just to heat the peas, ladle into bowls, and serve.

# honey mustard and mint chicken breasts

## makes 4 servings

## marinating time: 6 hours

Mustard and mint, you say? This is an easy and unique marinated chicken dish. A new twist for your barbecues and cookouts—who knew?!

2 cloves garlic, finely chopped
½ teaspoon kosher salt
¼ cup olive oil
2 tablespoons white balsamic vinegar
2 tablespoons Dijon mustard
1 teaspoon honey
2 tablespoons chopped fresh mint

1½ teaspoons dried oregano
½ teaspoon dried thyme leaves
½ teaspoon onion powder
¼ teaspoon freshly ground black pepper
4 (6-ounce) boneless, skinless chicken
   breasts

Place the garlic on a cutting board and sprinkle with the salt. Using the flat side of a knife, continuously apply pressure to the garlic and salt until a paste forms. Add the paste to a small bowl with the oil, vinegar, mustard, honey, mint, oregano, thyme, onion powder, and black pepper. Whisk until thoroughly blended. Add the marinade to a resealable bag along with the chicken and shake the bag to coat the chicken. Refrigerate for at least 6 hours and up to 2 days.

Remove the chicken from the refrigerator and let rest at room temperature for 30 minutes before grilling. Preheat a grill to medium-high heat and oil the grates. Place the chicken on the grill and cook for 4 to 6 minutes per side, until cooked through.

# grilled chicken and beer kebabs

## makes 4 servings

## marinating time: 4 hours

This is a great summer barbecue dish. Embellish it with chunks of green and red peppers, onions, and mushrooms to create an entire meal on a stick.

1 cup gluten-free beer
2 tablespoons freshly squeezed lemon juice
1 tablespoon olive oil
1 tablespoon spicy brown mustard
1 tablespoon gluten-free Worcestershire
  sauce
1 clove garlic, minced
1 tablespoon finely chopped fresh parsley

1 teaspoon paprika
1 teaspoon dried oregano
1 teaspoon kosher salt
⅛ teaspoon freshly ground black pepper
1½ pounds boneless, skinless chicken
  breasts, cut into 1-inch cubes
8 wooden skewers, soaked in water for
  20 minutes

In a medium bowl, whisk together the beer, lemon juice, olive oil, mustard, Worcestershire sauce, garlic, parsley, paprika, oregano, salt, and black pepper.

Place the chicken in a resealable plastic bag, add the marinade, and refrigerate for at least 4 hours or overnight.

Preheat a grill to medium-high heat and thread the marinated chicken pieces ¼ inch apart on the soaked skewers.

Lightly oil the hot grill rates and grill the kebabs for 4 to 5 minutes on each side, until cooked through.

# italian herb-crusted salmon

## makes 6 servings

This simple, flavorful seafood dish will be on your favorites list when you use this excellent bread crumb topping. Udi's gluten-free white bread blended in a food processor and mixed with seasonings and butter does it just right.

2 tablespoons honey
2 tablespoons Dijon mustard
½ teaspoon kosher salt
6 slices (about 5 ounces) Udi's gluten-free White Sandwich Bread
2 tablespoons finely chopped fresh parsley

2 teaspoons Italian seasoning
½ teaspoon garlic powder
¼ teaspoon freshly ground black pepper
1 tablespoon plus 1 teaspoon butter, melted
6 (6-ounce) salmon fillets

Preheat the oven to 350°F and grease a shallow baking pan.

In a small bowl, whisk together the honey, mustard, and salt. Set aside.

Place the bread in a food processor and blend into crumbs. Place the bread crumbs in a large bowl and mix in the parsley, Italian seasoning, garlic powder, pepper, and melted butter.

Place the salmon fillets in the prepared pan, brush generously with honey mustard, and coat with the bread crumb mixture. Bake for 15 to 20 minutes, until cooked through.

# pretzel-crusted tilapia
# with dijon cream sauce

## makes 4 to 6 servings

The newest craze for pretzel and mustard lovers—encrusting your favorite dinner item with the combination! Try these fresh tilapia fillets for a fabulous and novel entrée.

½ cup white rice flour
¼ teaspoon salt
⅛ teaspoon freshly ground black pepper
1 cup gluten-free pretzels (about 2 ounces)
½ cup gluten-free bread crumbs
½ teaspoon onion powder

2 eggs
1 tablespoon Dijon mustard
2 tablespoons olive oil
2 tablespoons unsalted butter
1 pound tilapia fillets
Dijon Cream Sauce (recipe follows)

In a shallow bowl, whisk together the white rice flour, salt, and pepper.

Using a food processor, blend together the pretzels, bread crumbs, and onion powder until fine crumbs form. Place on a shallow plate and set aside.

In another shallow bowl, whisk together the eggs and mustard.

Heat the oil and butter in a large skillet over medium-high heat.

Dredge both sides of the tilapia fillets in the seasoned flour, dip them in the egg mixture, and then coat them with the pretzel crumbs. Place in the pan and cook for 2 to 3 minutes on each side, until golden brown. Serve drizzled with Dijon cream sauce.

## dijon cream sauce (makes about 1¼ cups)

2 tablespoons butter
2 tablespoons minced shallot or onion
¼ cup white wine
2 tablespoons Dijon mustard

¾ cup heavy whipping cream or whole milk
1 teaspoon chopped fresh parsley (optional)
Salt and freshly ground black pepper

In a small saucepan, melt the butter over medium heat. Add the shallot and cook, stirring, for 1 to 2 minutes, until softened. Pour in the white wine and cook until reduced by half. Whisk in the mustard and cream and simmer for 2 to 3 minutes, until slightly thickened. Add the parsley and season to taste with salt and pepper.

# lemon butter crumb-topped cod

## makes 2 to 4 servings

This light and lemony fish is complete in about 20 minutes but will leave your family or guests thinking you slaved in the kitchen for hours.

4 tablespoons (½ stick) butter
2 tablespoons finely diced onion
½ cup finely diced celery
Grated zest and juice of 1 lemon

1 cup finely ground Rice Chex cereal
1 tablespoon finely chopped fresh parsley
⅛ teaspoon freshly ground black pepper
1 pound cod fillets

Preheat the oven to 350°F and grease a casserole dish.

In a medium sauté pan over medium-high heat, melt 2 tablespoons of the butter. Add the onion and celery and cook until tender, 2 to 3 minutes. Stir in the remaining 2 tablespoons butter, the lemon zest, juice, and ground cereal, and cook until the butter has been absorbed. Remove the pan from the heat and stir in the parsley and pepper.

Place the cod in the prepared casserole dish and spread a layer of the crumb mixture evenly over the top. Bake for 12 to 15 minutes, until the crumb topping is golden brown and the fish is cooked through.

ingredient alert: I recommend using gluten-free Rice Chex cereal made by General Mills.

# tortilla-crusted flounder with grilled pineapple salsa

## makes 4 to 6 servings

Here's another great way to jazz up your fish. Ground tortilla chips with cumin and garlic make a savory and crunchy coating, and the fish is topped with a grilled, sweet pineapple salsa to heighten the pizzazz.

1 pound flounder fillets
¼ pound (about 1½ cups) finely ground corn tortilla chips
¾ teaspoon garlic powder
½ teaspoon ground cumin
¼ cup white rice flour

¼ teaspoon kosher salt, plus more for seasoning
2 eggs
Olive oil, for frying
Grilled Pineapple Salsa (recipe follows)

Pat the fish fillets dry with paper towels and set aside.

Place the tortilla chips in a food processor with the garlic powder and cumin. Process until finely ground and place in a shallow bowl.

In a second bowl, whisk together the white rice flour and ¼ teaspoon of the salt.

In a third bowl, whisk the eggs until light and frothy.

In a large sauté pan, heat ¼ inch olive oil over medium-high heat.

Dredge both sides of the fish in the flour mixture, dip into the eggs, and then coat with the tortilla crumbs.

Fry the fish in the hot oil for 2 to 3 minutes on each side, until golden brown. Sprinkle lightly with kosher salt and serve with the salsa.

# grilled pineapple salsa (makes 4 cups)

1 (3- to 4-pound) pineapple, peeled and cut
   crosswise into ½-inch slices
1 tablespoon extra-virgin olive oil
¾ cup diced red bell pepper
¼ cup finely diced red onion

2 tablespoons finely chopped fresh cilantro
1 to 2 teaspoons diced seeded jalapeño
   pepper
1 tablespoon freshly squeezed lime juice
Kosher salt

Preheat a grill to medium-high heat and brush the pineapple slices with the olive oil. Place the pineapple on the hot grates and cook for 4 to 5 minutes on each side, until slightly charred and grill marked. Remove the pineapple from the grill and set aside to cool to room temperature.

Meanwhile, combine the red pepper, red onion, cilantro, jalapeño to taste, and lime juice in a medium bowl.

Dice the cooled pineapple, discarding the core, add to the bowl, and toss until mixed. Season with salt to taste.

chef's note: To save time, the salsa can be made with fresh pineapple that is not grilled.

# tangy grilled swordfish

## makes 4 servings

### marinating time: 4 hours

This zesty citrus marinade will work wonders on any of your favorite grilled fish. Try it with swordfish, salmon, or mahimahi.

2 tablespoons gluten-free soy sauce
2 tablespoons freshly squeezed orange juice
1 tablespoon ketchup
1 tablespoon olive oil
1 tablespoon chopped fresh parsley
1 clove garlic, minced
1 teaspoon sesame oil

½ teaspoon freshly squeezed lemon juice
¼ teaspoon dried oregano
¼ teaspoon freshly ground black pepper
Pinch of cayenne
1 pound swordfish fillets
Lemon and lime wedges, for garnish

In a medium bowl, whisk together the soy sauce, orange juice, ketchup, olive oil, parsley, garlic, sesame oil, lemon juice, oregano, pepper, and cayenne. Place the swordfish fillets in a large resealable plastic bag and pour the marinade over the fish. Release excess air from the bag, seal tightly, and refrigerate for at least 4 hours and up to overnight.

Preheat a grill to medium-high heat and oil the grates. Grill the fish for 3 to 4 minutes with the lid shut, then flip the fish over and grill for another 3 to 4 minutes, to the desired doneness. Serve with lemon and lime wedges.

# turkey and tart apple meat loaf

## makes 6 servings

### cooking time: 45 to 50 minutes

The turkey and tart apples make a much lighter, healthier, and more exciting version of the traditional meat loaf. Serve with your favorite mashed potatoes to make a fantastic comfort meal for a real meat and potato lover's delight.

1 tablespoon olive oil
1½ cups finely diced onions
5 cloves garlic, minced
1 cup diced Granny Smith apple
½ teaspoon dried thyme leaves
2 pounds ground turkey
½ cup chopped fresh parsley
½ cup light cream or half-and-half
¼ cup ketchup

2 teaspoons gluten-free Worcestershire sauce
2 eggs
1½ cups gluten-free Italian-seasoned bread crumbs
1 teaspoon salt
½ teaspoon freshly ground black pepper
¼ cup apple smoked barbecue sauce

Preheat the oven to 350°F and grease a 9 by 5-inch loaf pan.

In a sauté pan over medium-high heat, heat the olive oil. Add the onions and garlic and cook, stirring, for 4 to 5 minutes, until tender. Add the apple and thyme and cook for another 2 minutes. Remove from the heat and set aside.

In a large bowl, use your hands to mix together the turkey, parsley, cream, ketchup, Worcestershire sauce, eggs, bread crumbs, salt, pepper, and apple mixture.

Pack into a loaf pan, brush the barbecue sauce over the top, and bake for 45 to 50 minutes, until the internal temperature reads 165°F on an instant-read thermometer. Let rest for 10 minutes before slicing and serving.

chef's note: If you can't find apple smoked barbecue sauce, substitute your favorite barbecue sauce.

# creole sausage and shrimp with creamy grits

## makes 4 servings

When visiting New Orleans, I fell in love with both its culture and its cuisine. The hot and spicy shrimp is offset by the creamy grits—a very typical Creole combination.

1 pound medium shrimp, peeled and deveined
2½ to 3 teaspoons Creole seasoning
2 tablespoons olive oil
½ pound andouille sausage, diced
1 tablespoon butter
¼ cup minced onion
¼ cup minced celery

¼ cup minced red bell pepper
½ cup gluten-free chicken broth
¼ cup canned diced tomatoes, drained
3 tablespoons whole-grain mustard
1 teaspoon gluten-free Worcestershire sauce
½ cup light cream or half-and-half
Salt and freshly ground black pepper
Creamy Grits (recipe follows)

Pat the shrimp dry with paper towels. In a medium bowl, toss the shrimp with the Creole seasoning until coated; set aside.

Heat the olive oil in a large skillet over medium-high heat. Add the sausage and cook for about 5 minutes, until lightly browned. Using a slotted spoon, transfer the sausage to a bowl and set aside.

Add the shrimp to the pan and cook for 2 to 3 minutes, until just cooked through. Transfer to the bowl with the sausage and let rest.

Melt the butter in the same pan and add the onion, celery, and red pepper. Cook for 2 to 3 minutes, until tender. Whisk in the chicken broth, tomatoes, mustard, Worcestershire sauce, and cream. Simmer until the sauce thickens, about 5 minutes. Add the sausage and shrimp, simmer for another minute, and season with salt and pepper to taste. Serve over the hot grits.

# creamy grits

**2 cups gluten-free chicken broth**
**½ cup gluten-free corn grits**
**2 tablespoons cream**

**4 tablespoons (½ stick) butter**
**Salt and freshly ground black pepper**

In a medium saucepan over medium-high heat, bring the chicken broth to a boil. Slowly whisk in the corn grits, lower the heat to medium, and, whisking frequently, cook the grits for 15 minutes, until thickened and tender. Stir in the cream and butter and season with salt and pepper to taste.

# golden walnut baked stuffed shrimp

## makes 6 to 8 servings

Jumbo shrimp packed with a seafood stuffing made with fresh crab, walnuts, golden crackers, butter, and white wine—delectable!

½ cup walnuts, crushed
1 (4.4-ounce) box Glutino Original Crackers (about 32 crackers), crushed
6 tablespoons butter
2 tablespoons minced celery

½ pound crabmeat
¼ cup white wine
1 pound (16 to 20 count) shrimp, peeled and deveined, tails on

In a large bowl, stir together the walnuts and crackers.

In a medium sauté pan over medium-high heat, melt 3 tablespoons of the butter. Add the celery and cook for 1 minute. Add the remaining butter and the crabmeat. Cook for 5 minutes, until the crabmeat is cooked, and then add the mixture to the walnut-cracker mixture. Add the white wine and stir until thoroughly combined. Refrigerate to cool before stuffing into the shrimp.

Preheat the oven to 400°F.

Butterfly the shrimp and place on a baking sheet. Place 1 rounded tablespoon of stuffing on each shrimp. Bake for 15 to 20 minutes, until the shrimp are pink.

# buttery herb-crumbed scallops and mushrooms

## makes 6 to 8 servings

The day I made this dish my wife went into labor with our third son, Stephen. I pulled them out of the oven and placed them on the stove to cool as we were running out the door. I told my father-in-law to try a few bites of the buttery scallop dish and let me know what he thought before I'd add the recipe to the book. Not only did he try it; he ate the entire pan!

1 pound bay scallops
¼ teaspoon kosher salt
⅛ teaspoon freshly ground black pepper
3 tablespoons butter, plus more for coating the pie plate
1 clove garlic, minced
1 cup chopped mushrooms (about 3 ounces)

¼ cup dry sherry
½ cup gluten-free bread crumbs
½ cup finely ground gluten-free Glutino Original Crackers (about 2 ounces)
2 tablespoons chopped fresh parsley
1½ tablespoons freshly squeezed lemon juice

Preheat the oven to 400°F and butter a 9-inch pie plate.

Place the scallops in the prepared pie plate and sprinkle with the salt and pepper.

Melt 3 tablespoons of the butter in a large sauté pan over medium-high heat. Add the garlic and mushrooms and cook, stirring, for 1 to 2 minutes, until the mushrooms are tender. Add the sherry and allow to simmer for 1 minute. Stir in the bread crumbs, cracker crumbs, and parsley and cook until lightly crisp, 3 to 4 minutes.

Top the scallops with the crumb topping, sprinkle with the lemon juice, and bake for 12 to 15 minutes, until golden brown.

# gramma nancy's stuffed peppers

## makes 6 to 8 servings

### cooking time: 1 hour

Giant sweet red peppers overflowing with a juicy mixture of ground beef, rice, tomatoes, and Parmesan and baked until hot and delicious, served with a salad and glass of red wine, make for a perfect comfort food meal for a cool fall night.

1 tablespoon salt
4 large red bell peppers, halved lengthwise and seeded
1 cup long-grain brown rice
6 large tomatoes, cored and chopped
¼ cup finely chopped fresh parsley
¼ cup finely chopped fresh basil
2 tablespoons chopped garlic
2 pounds ground beef

1 cup diced green bell pepper
1¼ cups diced yellow onion
1 teaspoon kosher salt
¼ teaspoon freshly ground black pepper
¼ cup finely grated Parmesan cheese, plus extra for sprinkling
¼ cup ketchup
1 tablespoon gluten-free Worcestershire sauce

Preheat the oven to 350°F. Oil a baking dish large enough to hold all the stuffed pepper halves.

Place the salt in a large pot of water and bring to a boil over high heat. Add the red peppers and cook for 2 to 3 minutes, until the flesh softens. Drain and set aside.

Cook the rice according to the package directions.

In a medium saucepan over medium-high heat, simmer the tomatoes, parsley, basil, and garlic for 15 to 20 minutes.

In a large skillet over medium-high heat, cook the ground beef, green pepper, onion, salt, and pepper until the meat is evenly browned and cooked through.

In a large bowl, thoroughly mix together the ground beef mixture, tomato mixture, cooked brown rice, ¼ cup of the Parmesan cheese, the ketchup, and the Worcestershire sauce.

Arrange the peppers cut side up in the prepared baking dish and spoon generous amounts of filling into the peppers. Sprinkle Parmesan cheese on top of the peppers and bake for 35 to 40 minutes, until hot in the center.

# pistachio-and-mustard-encrusted lamb chops

## makes 4 to 6 servings

This features a surprisingly delicious blend of pistachios and honey mustard on succulent lamb chops. Use your china and your best silverware for a fine dining experience or pick them up and eat them as a lamb chop lollipop appetizer. Either way, they're seriously amazing.

1 (1½-pound) rack of lamb, frenched and cut into individual chops
Salt and freshly ground black pepper
1 tablespoon olive oil

¼ cup honey mustard
4 garlic cloves, finely chopped
½ cup dry-roasted pistachios
1 tablespoon cornstarch

Preheat the oven to 400°F. Grease a baking sheet.

Sprinkle the lamb chops lightly with salt and pepper.

Heat the olive oil in a large skillet over medium-high heat and sear the chops for about 1 minute on each side. Place on the prepared pan to cool.

In a shallow bowl, mix together the honey mustard and garlic.

Using a food processor, blend together the pistachios, cornstarch, ⅛ teaspoon salt, and a pinch of black pepper until coarsely ground. Pour into a second shallow bowl. Using a spoon or spatula, spread a layer of mustard on one side of each chop and then press it into the pistachios so that they adhere to the mustard. Place the chops back on the oiled pan with the crust facing up and bake for 8 to 10 minutes, until an instant-read thermometer reads 140°F for medium-rare. Serve immediately.

# plum barbecued baby back ribs

## makes 6 to 8 servings

### marinating time: overnight

### cook time: 4 1/2 hours

This fruity plum sauce makes for succulent, mouthwatering, finger-licking-good baby back ribs.

**Dry Rub (recipe follows)**
**6 pounds pork baby back ribs**
**Plum Sauce (recipe follows)**

Using your hands, massage the dry rub mixture into both sides of the ribs until evenly coated. Cover with plastic wrap and refrigerate overnight.

Preheat the oven to 200°F and line a baking sheet with aluminum foil.

Place the ribs on a rack on the lined pan and bake for 4 hours. Remove the ribs from the oven and allow to cool slightly. Preheat a grill to medium heat.

Brush the plum sauce over the ribs and cook on the grill for 30 minutes, turning the ribs every 10 minutes while brushing with plum sauce.

## dry rub (makes about ¾ cup)

**3 tablespoons ground allspice**
**3 tablespoons brown sugar**
**3 tablespoons garlic powder**
**1 tablespoon kosher salt**

**1 teaspoon freshly ground nutmeg**
**1 teaspoon ground cinnamon**
**1 teaspoon dried thyme leaves**
**1 teaspoon dry mustard**

In a medium mixing bowl, combine all the dry rub ingredients and stir until thoroughly blended. The rub can be stored tightly sealed in the refrigerator for up to 4 weeks.

# plum sauce (makes 2½ cups)

½ cup plum jam
½ cup white vinegar
½ cup ketchup
¼ cup honey

2 tablespoons minced garlic
¼ cup freshly squeezed lime juice
1 tablespoon minced sweet onion
½ cup plum wine

To make the plum sauce: In a saucepan over medium heat, heat the jam, vinegar, ketchup, honey, garlic, lime juice, and onion until the sauce boils. Add the plum wine and let the sauce simmer for 5 minutes before removing from the heat and allowing it to cool to room temperature. If making ahead, refrigerate in a tightly sealed container until ready to use. It will keep for up to 1 week.

# spinach and ricotta cheese eggplant roulades

## makes 4 to 6 servings

### baking time: 35 to 40 minutes

Grampa nearly devoured the whole pan of these savory and filling eggplant roulades. The very thinly sliced eggplant stuffed with spinach, Parmesan, ricotta, and basil pesto, covered in bread crumbs and drenched in a marinara sauce, makes for a delightful alternative to stuffed shells or manicotti.

Olive oil, for frying
½ cup finely diced onion
2 cloves garlic, minced
6 ounces fresh baby spinach
1 cup ricotta cheese
½ cup finely grated Parmesan cheese
¼ cup basil pesto
1 egg

1 cup marinara or tomato sauce
½ cup white rice flour
½ teaspoon salt
¼ teaspoon freshly ground black pepper
1½ pounds eggplant
½ cup shredded mozzarella cheese
¼ cup gluten-free bread crumbs

In a large sauté pan over medium heat, heat 1 tablespoon of the olive oil, add the onion and garlic, and cook, stirring, for 3 minutes. Add the spinach and cook for 3 to 4 minutes, until wilted. Transfer the spinach mixture to a large bowl and let cool.

In a small bowl, mix together the ricotta, ¼ cup of the Parmesan, the basil pesto, egg, and cooled spinach mixture. Cover and refrigerate.

Preheat the oven to 375°F, lightly grease a 9 by 13-inch baking dish, and line a baking sheet with paper towels. Evenly spread ½ cup of the marinara sauce over the bottom of the prepared baking dish.

On a shallow plate, mix together the white rice flour, salt, and pepper. Peel and slice the eggplant lengthwise into ¼-inch-thick slices.

In a large skillet over medium-high heat, heat ⅛ inch of oil. Dredge the eggplant slices in the flour mixture, add to the pan a few at a time, and cook for 1 minute on each side. Transfer the eggplant slices to the paper towels on the baking sheet as they are cooked.

Spread 2 tablespoons of the ricotta-spinach filling on each slice of cooked eggplant and roll up into roulades. Place the roulades on top of the sauce in the baking dish and top with the remaining ½ cup of the marinara. Sprinkle the top with the remaining ¼ cup Parmesan, the mozzarella, and the bread crumbs. Spray with cooking spray a sheet of aluminum foil large enough to cover the pan and cover the dish tightly. Bake for 20 minutes, remove the foil, and bake for another 15 to 20 minutes, until the cheese is golden brown. Let stand for 5 minutes before serving.

# the udi-tella

## makes 4 to 6 servings

This sandwich consists of a fabulous combination of chocolate hazelnut spread and bananas, grilled between two pieces of Udi's whole-grain bread. I gave out samples of these as a last-minute creation at a conference in Boston, and it was difficult to keep up with the demand! These rate a definite "WOW!"

12 slices Udi's Whole Grain Bread
6 tablespoons Nutella chocolate hazelnut
   spread

1 banana, cut into 24 thin slices
Butter, for toasting

Place 6 slices of the bread on a flat surface and spread 1 tablespoon Nutella evenly on each one. Place 4 banana slices on the chocolate and top with the other slice of bread. Heat a ridged grill pan or a skillet over medium-high heat and coat with melted butter. Place the sandwiches in the pan and grill until golden brown on the bottom. Flip over and cook the second side until golden brown. Enjoy!

# international flavors

When asked which nation he preferred to dine in, a renowned and well-traveled chef once answered that he most liked to eat in the restaurants of the United States. When asked why, he stated simply that when in Italy you get Italian food, when visiting France you get French cuisine, but when traveling across America, the food choices are boundless and menu options offer dishes of nearly every country in the world. And he was so right!

At my present job, I work with men and women from at least fifteen different countries, including Mexico, China, Thailand, Italy, and Germany. One of the great benefits of being surrounded by such diversity is the authentic cultural education it affords and the preferences and recipes that are joyfully shared. These are dishes that are favorites of real people, often passed down from generation to generation, and typically beyond delicious. I am grateful to the many people who have shared their secrets for this chapter.

I hereby admit to being a cooking show junkie and to being especially addicted to watching those chefs who travel the world preparing and eating unique and interesting dishes native to different regions. As someone who would try eating any food at least once, these shows keep me riveted and confirm for me how we Americans often view food as more of an adventure than just a meal. With all this in mind, I set out in this chapter to develop recipes with truly enticing international flavors that are still completely gluten free.

Having an Italian heritage, I just had to create gluten-free versions of Beef Steak Milanese and Chicken Romano. For everyone who loved the Mexican dishes in my last cookbook, I offer my Chubby Chicken Enchiladas, a soon-to-be favorite. I want to specifically thank the country of Switzerland for that classic dish that became a focal point of entertaining during the sixties and seventies—Cheese Fondue. It's true—you can fire up that old fondue pot again and make a truly delicious and gluten-free beer-flavored cheese fondue to saturate and soak over chunks of toasted bagels—ah, the memories! And I send gratitude to my coworker, Angel, whose great love for pork inspired me to create the Grilled Mojo Pork Tenderloin. Also included in this chapter are such favorites as Shrimp Egg Rolls, straight off the pupu platter, crunchy on the outside and full of sweet tender shrimp and vegetables on the inside. This chapter was really a favorite of mine to work on, and from around the world and my own dining room table I encourage you all to "Mangia-mangia!" and Bon Appétit!

# chicken romano

## makes 4 to 6 servings

## cooking time: 25 to 30 minutes

A classic "Roman" chicken dish, made with the highest-quality Italian cheeses, is an excellent supper dish when served with your favorite risotto or a chunk of hot, crusty, gluten-free bread.

8 tablespoons (1 stick) butter, melted
2 cloves garlic, minced
1 tablespoon Dijon mustard
2 teaspoons gluten-free Worcestershire sauce
1 cup plain gluten-free bread crumbs
2 tablespoons finely grated pecorino Romano cheese

2 tablespoons finely grated Parmesan cheese
2 teaspoons finely chopped fresh parsley
1½ pounds boneless, skinless chicken breasts, butterflied

Preheat the oven to 350°F and grease a baking sheet.

In a medium shallow dish, whisk together the butter, garlic, mustard, and Worcestershire sauce.

In a separate shallow dish, mix together the bread crumbs, Romano cheese, Parmesan cheese, and parsley.

Dip the chicken into the butter mixture, coating both sides, and then into the bread crumb mixture. Place on the greased pan and bake for 25 to 30 minutes, until the chicken is cooked through.

**variation:** In a small bowl, combine ⅓ cup finely chopped fresh spinach, 1 tablespoon finely chopped fresh basil, and ¼ cup shredded mozzarella cheese. Place on the chicken breasts during the last 5 minutes of cooking.

# beef steak milanese

## makes 4 to 6 servings

Here's a traditional Italian entrée that will please anyone. Your friends will rave about this sumptuous and tender breaded steak cutlet topped with sweet tomatoes, peppery arugula, and fresh Parmesan cheese.

4 plum tomatoes
¼ cup diced red onion
¾ cup fresh basil leaves, finely chopped
3 cups lightly packed baby arugula
¼ cup finely grated Parmesan cheese,
    plus ¼ cup freshly shaved Parmesan
2 eggs
2 tablespoons plus 1 tablespoon extra-virgin

olive oil
1 pound beef cube steaks
1 tablespoon freshly squeezed lemon juice
¼ teaspoon salt
¼ teaspoon freshly ground black pepper
½ cup gluten-free plain bread crumbs

In a medium bowl, combine the tomatoes, onion, basil, arugula, and shaved Parmesan. Set aside.

In a shallow bowl, beat the eggs until light and frothy.

In a second bowl, combine the bread crumbs and grated Parmesan cheese.

In a skillet over medium-high heat, heat 2 tablespoons of the olive oil. Dredge the cube steaks in the egg mixture, allow the excess to drip off, and then dip into the bread crumb mixture, coating both sides. Add to the skillet and cook for 3 minutes, until lightly browned, before turning over and cooking for another 3 to 4 minutes.

In a small bowl, whisk together the remaining 1 tablespoon of olive oil, the lemon juice, salt, and pepper. Add to the arugula salad and toss until thoroughly coated.

Place the cooked steak on a platter and top with the arugula salad.

# grilled mojo pork tenderloin

## makes 4 to 6 servings

*Mojo* is the catchall Latin American name for several types of sauces varying in flavors and spiciness. Mojo sauce is commonly served over meats and potatoes, but it can also flavor anything from tomatoes to peppers to avocado. In Cuban cooking mojo applies to any sauce that is made with garlic, olive oil, and a citrus juice (traditionally sour orange). As in this recipe, it is commonly used to accompany pork. This grilled version is an excellent alternative to common cookout fare.

2 pork tenderloins (about 2 pounds)
1 tablespoon olive oil
½ teaspoon kosher salt

½ teaspoon freshly ground black pepper
1½ teaspoons fresh oregano or ½ teaspoon dried
Mojo Sauce (recipe follows)

Preheat a grill to medium heat.

Rub the pork tenderloin thoroughly with olive oil and sprinkle with salt, pepper, and oregano. Grill for 12 to 15 minutes, turning occasionally, until the pork reaches 145°F on an instant-read thermometer.

Let the pork rest on a cutting board for 5 minutes before slicing ½ inch thick. Place the slices on a serving platter and spoon the sauce over the pork just before serving.

## mojo sauce (makes about 1 cup)

¼ cup extra-virgin olive oil
½ cup freshly squeezed orange juice
¼ cup freshly squeezed lime juice
½ cup chopped fresh cilantro
8 cloves garlic, minced
2 teaspoons ground cumin

2 tablespoons fresh oregano or 2 teaspoons dried
1 jalapeño pepper, seeded and minced (optional)
Salt and freshly ground black pepper

In a medium bowl, whisk together the olive oil, orange juice, lime juice, cilantro, garlic, cumin, oregano, and jalapeño. Season with salt and black pepper to taste. Set aside for about 20 minutes to allow the flavors to meld together. Just before spooning over the pork, whisk the sauce a second time. Leftover sauce can be refrigerated in an airtight container for up to 1 week and used on meats, seafood, poultry, vegetables, and potatoes.

# chubby chicken enchiladas

## makes 4 to 6 servings

### cooking time: 45 to 50 minutes

You can quickly transform simple chicken breasts into a Mexican fiesta just by adding fajita seasoning, green chiles, onions, salsa, and cheese. To save time, the chicken can be cooked a day before and refrigerated until needed.

1 pound boneless, skinless chicken breast
2 teaspoons olive oil
1 tablespoon taco or fajita seasoning
1 cup sour cream
1 (4-ounce) can diced green chiles
½ cup chopped green onions
¼ cup finely chopped fresh cilantro
½ cup plus ¼ cup shredded sharp cheddar
   cheese

½ cup plus ¼ cup shredded Monterey Jack
   cheese
1 teaspoon freshly squeezed lime juice
¾ teaspoon ground cumin
6 brown rice or corn tortillas
1 cup salsa

Preheat a grill to medium heat.

Place the chicken in a shallow dish, drizzle with olive oil, and sprinkle both sides evenly with the taco seasoning. Grill the chicken until an instant-read thermometer reaches 165°F. Set aside to cool.

Preheat the oven to 350°F and grease a 13 by 9-inch baking dish.

In a large bowl, stir together the sour cream, green chiles, green onions, cilantro, ½ cup of the cheddar cheese, ½ cup of the Monterey Jack cheese, the lime juice, and the cumin.

Dice the chicken and stir it into the sour cream mixture.

Place a tortilla on a flat surface, scoop ½ cup of the filling across the middle of the tortilla, and roll it up like a cigar. Place the filled enchiladas in the prepared baking dish seam side down. Top evenly with salsa, cover the pan with aluminum foil, and bake for 35 to 40 minutes, until cooked through.

Remove the foil, sprinkle with the remaining ¼ cup of each cheese, and bake for 5 to 10 minutes, until the cheese is melted. Serve immediately.

chef's note: If you don't have a grill, the chicken can be pan fried in 2 tablespoons of oilve oil over medium heat for 3 to 4 minutes per side until cooked through.

# shrimp egg rolls

## makes 18

## cooking time: 45 to 50 minutes

Finally, a gluten-free egg roll recipe that is crunchy and tasty, filled with shrimp and seasoned vegetables. These are both delicious and fun to make. Get your kids or friends to help you roll them up—tell them sharing the work makes the end product taste even better! Pair with a Chinese rice or noodle dish and your meal is complete.

### Filling
¼ cup vegetable oil
1 cup minced yellow onion
½ cup finely chopped celery
2 cloves garlic, minced
½ pound shrimp, peeled, deveined, and minced
1 (14-ounce) bag coleslaw mix
2 green onions, finely chopped
1 teaspoon freshly minced ginger, or ½ teaspoon ground ginger
1 tablespoon gluten-free soy sauce
1 tablespoon sugar
1 tablespoon toasted sesame oil

### Wrappers
½ cup white rice flour
¼ cup tapioca flour
¼ cup cornstarch
½ teaspoon xanthan gum
Pinch of salt
1¼ cups milk
6 tablespoons water
2 eggs plus 1 egg, beaten
2 tablespoons butter, melted
1 tablespoon vegetable shortening, melted

Vegetable oil, for deep frying

To make the filling: Heat 2 tablespoons of the vegetable oil in a skillet over medium-high heat. Add the onion, celery, and garlic and cook, stirring, for 2 to 3 minutes, until tender. Add the shrimp and cook, stirring occasionally, for about 5 minutes, until the shrimp turns pink.

Remove the shrimp mixture from the pan and place in a large mixing bowl. Place the skillet back on the heat and add the remaining 2 tablespoons vegetable oil. Add the coleslaw mix, green onions, and ginger and cook,

stirring, for 1 minute. Add the soy sauce, sugar, and sesame oil and cook for 5 minutes, stirring occasionally. Add to the bowl with the shrimp, mix thoroughly, and set aside to cool slightly.

To make the wrappers: In a small bowl, sift together the white rice flour, tapioca flour, cornstarch, xanthan gum, and salt.

In a blender, process the milk, water, 2 of the eggs, the melted butter, melted shortening, and flour mixture until all ingredients are completely blended.

Heat a 10-inch nonstick pan over medium heat. Spray the pan with nonstick cooking spray and pour 2 tablespoons of the batter in the center of the pan, rocking the pan to swirl the batter into a thin disk. Cook for 30 to 40 seconds, flip, and cook for another 10 to 15 seconds. Place the wrapper on a platter to cool and continue making wrappers with the remaining batter.

To assemble the egg rolls: Drain excess liquid from the filling by transferring it to a strainer. Place a wrapper on a flat surface and place 2 tablespoons of the filling in the center. Using a brush, dampen the top edges of the wrapper with the beaten egg and roll the bottom (closest to you) over the filling. Fold in the sides of the wrapper and continue rolling up until the egg roll is closed, pressing the seams to seal it tightly. Set the egg roll aside and continue making egg rolls until all the filling and wrappers are used up.

To fry the egg rolls: Fill a saucepan halfway with vegetable oil and heat over medium-high heat to 360°F on a deep-fat thermometer. Preheat the oven to 400°F.

Using tongs, place an egg roll seam side down in the hot oil, holding it closed with the tongs for 5 seconds before releasing it into the oil. Fry for 3 to 5 minutes, until golden brown, and place on paper towels to drain. More than one egg roll can be cooked at a time.

After all the egg rolls are fried, place them on a baking pan and bake for 10 minutes. Serve with your favorite dipping sauce.

# kickin' paella

## makes 6 to 8 servings

### cooking time: 1 hour

This paella is a spectacular mixture of some of the finest ingredients. Chorizo sausage, shrimp, mussels, chicken, and vegetables are mixed with rice and just the right spices to make a colorful party dish.

6 tablespoons olive oil
8 chicken thighs
1½ teaspoons plus 1 teaspoon salt
1 pound gluten-free dry chorizo sausage,
    sliced into half-moons
2 cups chopped onion
2 cups diced red bell pepper
1½ cups diced green bell pepper
3 tablespoons minced garlic
2 teaspoons saffron threads

1 teaspoon dried thyme leaves
1 teaspoon paprika
¼ teaspoon cayenne
4 cups gluten-free chicken broth
2 cups medium-grain rice
1 pound large shrimp, peeled and deveined
¾ pound mussels, cleaned
2 cups frozen green peas, thawed
¼ cup chopped fresh parsley
Salt and freshly ground black pepper

In a skillet or paella pan over medium-high heat, heat 3 tablespoons of the olive oil. Season the chicken thighs with 1 teaspoon of the salt and place in the oil skin side down. Cook the chicken for about 10 minutes on each side, until golden brown. Remove the chicken, allow to cool slightly, and then remove the skin and bones from the meat.

Add the remaining 3 tablespoons of olive oil to the pan along with the chorizo and cook for 8 to 10 minutes, until the sausage begins to caramelize. Add the onions, red peppers, and green peppers and continue to cook for about 5 minutes, until softened. Add the

garlic, saffron, thyme, paprika, cayenne, and chicken. Add the chicken broth and bring to a boil. Reduce the heat to medium, stir in the rice, and cook for 15 to 20 minutes, until the rice absorbs some of the liquid.

Nestle the shrimp and mussels into the rice and cook for about 5 minutes, until the shrimp turn pink and the mussels begin to open. Add the peas and parsley and cook for another 5 to 10 minutes, until the chicken broth is absorbed and the rice begins to form a crust on the bottom. Season with salt and pepper to taste.

# broccoli and chicken alfredo

## makes 4 to 6 servings

## cooking time: 45 to 50 minutes

This is a classic Italian combination of chicken and broccoli, cooked with cream and Parmesan cheese and ladled over thick fettuccine noodles. Mangia!

¾ pound gluten-free fettuccine
3 cups broccoli florets
1 pound boneless, skinless chicken breast, cut into ½-inch pieces
Salt and freshly ground black pepper
1 tablespoon olive oil

4 tablespoons (½ stick) unsalted butter
1½ cups half-and-half or whole milk
Pinch of freshly ground nutmeg
1¼ cups finely grated Parmesan cheese
½ teaspoon grated lemon zest

Cook the pasta according to the package directions, adding the broccoli during the last 3 minutes of cooking time. Drain and set aside.

Generously season the chicken with salt and pepper.

In a large pot, heat the olive oil over medium-high heat. Add the chicken and cook for about 5 minutes, until lightly browned and cooked through. Transfer the chicken to a bowl and let rest.

Meanwhile, melt the butter in a pot and slowly whisk in the half-and-half and nutmeg. When the cream is hot, whisk in the Parmesan cheese and simmer for about 5 minutes, until the sauce begins to thicken.

Add the chicken, pasta, broccoli, and lemon zest, tossing until the noodles are completely coated. Season with salt and pepper to taste.

chef's note: When draining pasta, reserve ½ cup of the pasta water. If the Alfredo sauce is too thick, add some of the pasta water to thin it out.

# cheese fondue

## makes 4 to 6 servings

It's true! You can fire up that old fondue pot again and make a delicious gluten-free beer-flavored cheese fondue to dip chunks of toasted Udi's bagels. Ah, the memories!

½ pound Gruyère cheese, grated
   (about 2 cups)
½ pound Emmentaler cheese, grated
   (about 2 cups)
1 tablespoon cornstarch
½ teaspoon dry mustard
1 clove garlic, halved

1 cup gluten-free beer or white wine
1 tablespoon freshly squeezed lemon juice
Pinch of freshly ground black pepper
Pinch of freshly ground nutmeg
Assorted dippers, such as Udi's Bagels,
   cut into cubes, broccoli florets, and
   cauliflower florets

In a large bowl, toss together the Gruyère cheese, Emmentaler cheese, cornstarch, and dry mustard. Set aside.

Rub the cut garlic clove on the bottom and sides of a medium saucepan. Add the beer and lemon juice and place over medium heat.

When the beer begins to simmer, add one small handful of cheese at a time to the beer, stirring until melted (do not boil). Continue until all the cheese is melted into the beer and then season with pepper and nutmeg. Pour into a fondue pot and serve with assorted dippers.

# chinese chicken and vegetables

## makes 4 to 6 servings

While Chinese food is a favorite in our home, it also makes for a sharp point of contention—a never-ending battle over brown sauce versus white. While I prefer the tangy richness of dark soy sauces, my wife gravitates toward the lighter, and typically safer, gluten-free white sauces. This recipe is a wonderfully surprising compromise, full of color, pungent, and pleasing to all.

2 tablespoons plus 1 tablespoon gluten-free soy sauce
3 tablespoons plus 1 tablespoon cornstarch
1 pound boneless, skinless chicken breast, cut into ¼-inch slices
1 tablespoon rice wine vinegar
1½ cups gluten-free chicken broth
2 tablespoons vegetable oil

1 tablespoon toasted sesame oil
1 cup sliced white button mushrooms
1 cup carrot matchsticks
1 cup snow peas
1 cup thinly sliced red bell pepper
1 (15-ounce) can baby corn, drained
½ cup finely sliced celery
Salt and freshly ground black pepper
2 cups cooked white rice

In a large bowl, whisk together 2 tablespoons of the soy sauce and 1 tablespoon of the cornstarch. Add the chicken, toss to coat with the sauce, and set aside.

In a medium bowl, whisk together the vinegar, chicken broth, remaining tablespoon of soy sauce, and remaining 3 tablespoons cornstarch.

In a wok or large skillet over medium-high heat, heat the vegetable and sesame oils. Add the chicken and cook for 4 to 5 minutes, stirring constantly, until the chicken is cooked. Add the mushrooms, carrots, peas, red pepper, corn, and celery and cook for 3 to 4 minutes, until the vegetables are tender. Stir in the chicken broth mixture, coating all the ingredients, and cook until the sauce thickens. Season with salt and pepper to taste and serve over white rice.

# pancetta, sausage, and mozzarella stuffing

## makes 12 to 14 servings

## cooking time: 1 hour

Over the years I've received repeated requests to come up with a gluten-free version of someone's cherished Thanksgiving stuffing recipe. This Italian classic with pancetta, hot and sweet sausages, mozzarella cheese, and Udi's Whole Grain Bread gets it just right.

8 tablespoons (1 stick) plus 2 tablespoons unsalted butter

12 slices Udi's Whole Grain Bread

1 tablespoon olive oil

¾ pound pancetta, cut into ½-inch dice

3 medium onions, halved and sliced

6 stalks celery, cut into ½-inch dice (about 3 cups)

1 pound sweet Italian sausage, casings removed

1 pound hot Italian sausage, casings removed

2 teaspoons ground dried thyme or 2 tablespoons fresh

1 teaspoon ground dried sage or 1 tablespoon fresh

2 teaspoons finely chopped fresh rosemary

1 pound mozzarella cheese, cut into ½-inch cubes

1 cup gluten-free chicken broth

1 cup hazelnuts, toasted and finely ground (page 182)

Salt and freshly ground black pepper

Preheat the oven to 350°F.

Using 8 tablespoons of the butter, spread the butter on both sides of the bread, place on a baking sheet, and bake for 10 minutes; then flip and bake for an additional 8 minutes, until golden brown and crispy. Set aside to cool; then cut into 1-inch cubes and place in a large bowl.

In a medium skillet over medium heat, heat the olive oil and the pancetta, and cook for about 8 minutes, until crispy. Using a slotted spoon, remove the pancetta from the pan and drain on paper towels. Add to the cubed bread. Drain off all but 1 tablespoon of the fat from the pan, add 1 tablespoon of the remaining butter, and place the pan back on medium

heat. Add the onions and cook for about 10 minutes, until golden brown and caramelized. Add to the bowl with the bread. In the same pan, heat the remaining tablespoon of butter, add the celery, and cook for about 8 minutes, until tender. Add to the bowl with the bread.

In a separate pan over medium heat, cook the sausage, breaking it up into small pieces with a wooden spoon, for about 10 minutes, until cooked through. Add the sausage to the bread bowl with the thyme, sage, and rosemary. When the stuffing is cool, add the mozzarella, chicken broth, and hazelnuts, tossing until all the ingredients are incorporated. Season with salt and pepper to taste before stuffing into the turkey.

# thai coconut curried shrimp

## makes 4 to 6 servings

Red curry paste adds a hint of spice to the mild and aromatic coconut milk and brown-sugared shrimp. Serve with soft, fluffy rice or rice stick noodles to offset the heat in this delicious dish.

1 tablespoon peanut or canola oil
1 cup thinly sliced red onion
1 cup finely chopped green onion
3 tablespoons red curry paste
1 (14-ounce) can unsweetened
    coconut milk
1 cup gluten-free chicken broth
2 tablespoons Thai fish sauce
2 teaspoons brown sugar

2 teaspoons granulated sugar
1 cup diced tomato
2 pounds medium shrimp, peeled and
    deveined
½ cup finely chopped fresh cilantro
½ cup salted cashews, crushed
2 teaspoons freshly squeezed lime juice
Cooked white rice or rice stick noodles,
    for serving

In a large skillet over medium-high heat, heat the oil. Add the red onion and cook for 2 to 3 minutes, until softened. Add the green onion and red curry paste and cook for 1 minute. Stir in the coconut milk, chicken broth, fish sauce, brown sugar, and granulated sugar. Bring to a boil, add the tomato, and simmer for 1 to 2 minutes. Add the shrimp and simmer, stirring occasionally, for 2 to 3 minutes, until the shrimp turn pink and are cooked through. Remove from the heat and stir in the cilantro, cashews, and lime juice. Serve over cooked white rice or rice stick noodles.

chef's note: For Thai Coconut Curried Chicken, diced boneless raw or cooked chicken can be substituted in place of the shrimp.

# tangy thai baby back ribs

## makes 4 to 6 servings

### cooking time: 4½ hours

The bright and complex sweet-and-sour tastes of Thai cooking pair with smoky, spicy barbecue flavor in these unique and incredible baby back ribs.

3 pounds baby back ribs
1 teaspoon kosher salt
½ teaspoon freshly ground black pepper
¼ cup gluten-free soy sauce
¼ cup sweet chili sauce
¼ cup freshly squeezed lime juice
⅓ cup packed brown sugar

1 tablespoon gluten-free Thai fish sauce
1 teaspoon toasted sesame oil
1 tablespoon minced peeled fresh ginger
1 clove garlic, minced
¼ teaspoon hot red pepper flakes
¼ cup plus 1 tablespoon chopped fresh cilantro

Preheat the oven to 200°F and season both sides of the ribs with salt and pepper. Place the ribs on a greased baking sheet, cover with aluminum foil, and cook for 4 hours. Remove the ribs from the oven and set aside to cool.

In a medium saucepan over medium heat, whisk together the soy sauce, sweet chili sauce, lime juice, brown sugar, fish sauce, sesame oil, ginger, garlic, red pepper, and ¼ cup of the cilantro and simmer just until the sugar is melted and the sauce is slightly thickened. Remove from the heat and set aside to cool.

Preheat a grill to medium heat.

Brush some of the sauce on both sides of the ribs. Cook for 30 minutes, turning every 10 minutes and brushing with more sauce. Cut the ribs into sections, place on a platter, and sprinkle with the remaining tablespoon of cilantro.

chef's note: To save time the sauce can be made and the ribs precooked a day ahead of time and refrigerated until needed.

# creamy chicken marsala

## makes 4 servings

This superb chicken dish, made with Marsala, a fortified Sicilian wine, is simple to make yet sophisticated enough to serve at your most elegant dinner party, especially when accompanied by tender asparagus and pasta cooked al dente.

4 boneless, skinless chicken breasts
(about 1 pound)
¼ cup cornstarch
1 tablespoon tapioca flour
¼ teaspoon baking soda
Salt and freshly ground black pepper
2 tablespoons butter
3 tablespoons olive oil

1 tablespoon finely chopped onion or shallot
¼ teaspoon dried oregano
1 cup sliced white button or baby bella
mushrooms
½ cup Marsala wine
½ cup gluten-free chicken broth
¼ cup light cream or half-and-half
2 tablespoons chopped fresh parsley

Place each chicken breast on a flat surface and cut it in half horizontally. Put each piece between two sheets of plastic wrap and pound lightly with a mallet or small kitchen skillet until the chicken is ¼ inch thick.

In a shallow bowl, whisk together the cornstarch, tapioca flour, baking soda, ⅛ teaspoon salt, and ⅛ teaspoon pepper.

In a large sauté pan over medium-high heat, melt the butter in the olive oil. Dredge the chicken in the flour mixture and shake off the excess. Add the chicken breasts to the pan and cook until lightly browned, about 3 minutes on each side. Transfer the chicken to a plate and pour off the excess fat from the pan.

Return the pan to the heat and stir in the onion and oregano. Cook for 1 minute and then add the mushrooms. Cook the mushrooms for another minute and then add the wine, scraping the bottom of the pan for 20 seconds before stirring in the chicken broth and cream. Add the chicken back to the pan and simmer for 5 to 6 minutes while the sauce reduces and thickens. Season with salt and pepper to taste and garnish with parsley just before serving.

# pasta
# and rice

As the manager of culinary development at a large university in Connecticut, I get a very close look at trends in food service, the popularity of products and dishes, and what does and doesn't work at the commercial food level. Without a doubt, pasta and rice dishes have been and will always be very popular menu items among the masses, including most college students. As most of you know, most basic rice found at the local grocery store, whether white, brown, jasmine or Arborio, is naturally gluten free. It is, however, still important to read those labels, especially when it comes to rice mixes or boxed risotto. Some of these blends may contain dried chicken, beef, or vegetable stock that itself contains wheat or gluten. They may even have small pasta pieces made from wheat, such as orzo, blended into them.

Most impressive lately is the large variety of gluten-free pasta that is not only readily available online and at health food stores but is also slowly filling the shelves at local supermarkets. In addition to the increase in variety, the quality of many of these pastas is improving steadily. Gluten-free pastas are now available in white rice, brown rice, corn, quinoa, potato, soy, and blended flour mixtures. And nearly all can be found in different shapes and sizes, such as penne, shells, linguine, fettuccine, fusilli, tagliatelle, ziti, elbows, spaghetti, rotini, and even lasagna sheets. Furthermore, there is a new and burgeoning market to be found in fresh gluten-free pastas, found in the frozen section of our specialty food stores, including the likes of gnocchi, ravioli, manicotti, tortellini, and cavatelli. Recently, when my wife and I actually made it out to a restaurant to have dinner, I was pleasantly surprised when the waiter handed her a gluten-free menu offering real gluten-free pasta dishes with a variety of sauces and toppings. This is a big improvement over the usual plain grilled fish or chicken dishes to which these menus are often limited.

In this chapter I touch upon a number of rice and pasta creations that have been requested by you, the reader, as well as favorites that have been enjoyed all along in my own house. These include Parmesan Potato Gnocchi with Roasted Garlic Butter—a classic Italian dish originating from Tuscany that dates back to the 1300s. There is a reason this one has survived the ages! Also included is my wife's favorite summer dish, Spinach and Plum Tomato Pasta Sauté, a gluten-free ziti made with fresh, juicy plum tomatoes from our garden and tossed with Italian herbs and spinach in a light broth. This one is not only very tasty but also hearty and healthy. The Spicy Peanut Chicken Pasta Salad is loaded with colorful vegetables and a spicy Thai peanut dressing, it is guaranteed to make a huge hit at your next cookout.

The rice dishes include favorites that have been prepared successfully by many of the students who take my first-year cooking class, including Scallop and Shrimp Asiago Risotto. This is a creamy rice made with fresh buttery scallops and tender succulent shrimp, declared by one freshman girl to be "mmmmm, so good." The Gingered Chicken Fried Rice with Cashews, a Chinese food favorite, will leave your local Chinese restaurant with numerous empty seats, since it can now be prepared by you at home, easily and without any doubt about its gluten-free status. This chapter will also provide numerous options for creativity and variety, while you experiment with different types of pasta and rice tossed with your own favorite flavors, meats, vegetables, and sauces. Have fun and enjoy the gluten-free journey!

# spinach and plum tomato pasta sauté

## makes 4 to 6 servings

Another Italian classic, with pasta, tomatoes, beans, and cheese. Use vegetable broth to make it vegetarian.

¾ pound brown rice penne pasta
1 tablespoon olive oil
4 cloves garlic, finely chopped
1 (15-ounce) can white cannellini beans, drained and rinsed
5 plum tomatoes, chopped
1 cup canned diced tomatoes with juice

1 cup gluten-free vegetable or chicken broth
½ teaspoon dried oregano
1 tablespoon chopped fresh basil
1 (10-ounce) bag fresh spinach
½ cup finely grated Parmesan cheese
Salt and freshly ground black pepper

Cook the pasta according to the package directions, drain, and set aside.

In a large skillet over medium-high heat, heat the oil, add the garlic, and cook for 1 minute. Add the beans, plum tomatoes, canned tomatoes, broth, oregano, and basil.

Simmer for 5 minutes, add the spinach, and cook for about 1 minute, until just wilted.

Add the pasta and cheese and toss until thoroughly coated. Season with salt and pepper to taste and serve.

# gingered chicken fried rice with cashews

## makes 4 to 6 servings

This variation of chicken fried rice is more elaborate than the usual Chinese restaurant fare, adding ginger, vegetables, and cashews to make it a meal in itself.

1 tablespoon vegetable oil
1 tablespoon toasted sesame oil
½ cup finely diced onion
1 teaspoon minced peeled fresh ginger
½ pound boneless, skinless chicken, diced
½ cup finely diced celery
1 cup fresh bean sprouts
½ cup frozen peas, thawed
1 (8-ounce) can water chestnuts, drained

½ cup bamboo shoots, diced
½ cup sliced shiitake or white button
  mushrooms
3 cups cooked rice
3 tablespoons gluten-free soy sauce
3 green onions, finely diced
½ cup cashews
Salt and freshly ground black pepper

In a preheated wok or large skillet over medium-high heat, heat the vegetable oil and sesame oil. Add the onion and ginger and cook for 1 minute. Add the chicken and cook, stirring occasionally, for 2 to 3 minutes, until the chicken is cooked through. Add the celery, bean sprouts, and peas and cook for 1 to 2 minutes. Add the water chestnuts, bamboo shoots, and mushrooms and cook for another 1 to 2 minutes. Stir in the rice, soy sauce, and green onions and cook until the rice is hot and no longer white. Add the cashews and season with salt and pepper to taste. Transfer to a large bowl or platter and serve.

# spicy peanut chicken pasta salad

## makes 6 to 8 servings

This dish is full of crunchy vegetables and tender noodles tossed in a spicy peanut butter dressing. It can be served as a main course or as a satisfying side dish at your next picnic. Enjoy it at room temperature or served cold.

8 ounces gluten-free fettuccine
6 tablespoons creamy peanut butter (not all-natural)
¼ cup gluten-free chicken broth
3 tablespoons gluten-free soy sauce
3 tablespoons rice vinegar
1 tablespoon toasted sesame oil
1 tablespoon honey
1 tablespoon freshly squeezed lime juice
1 tablespoon minced peeled fresh ginger

1 teaspoon sugar
½ teaspoon cayenne
1 pound chicken, cooked and chopped or shredded
2 cups red bell pepper matchsticks
1 cup grated carrots
½ cup finely chopped green onions
½ cup drained sliced water chestnuts
¼ cup chopped fresh cilantro
¼ cup unsalted peanuts, crushed

Cook the pasta according to the package directions, rinse with cold water, and drain.

In a medium bowl, whisk together the peanut butter, chicken broth, soy sauce, rice vinegar, sesame oil, honey, lime juice, ginger, sugar, and cayenne. Set aside.

In a large bowl, combine the chicken, red peppers, carrots, green onions, water chestnuts, cilantro, and pasta. Add the dressing and toss until thoroughly mixed and coated with dressing. Serve at room temperature or chilled, topped with crushed peanuts.

# three-cheese penne, pea, and bacon bake

## makes 6 servings

## baking time: 30 to 40 minutes

My first cookbook contains a recipe for a traditional macaroni and cheese, which requires melting the cheese in simmering cream. Here is an expanded version that includes bacon and peas to make a more filling and complete meal. It's quick and easy with no stovetop preparation needed.

1 (12-ounce) box gluten-free penne pasta
½ cup finely grated Parmesan cheese
¼ cup gluten-free bread crumbs
1 tablespoon butter, melted, or olive oil
1 (12-ounce) can evaporated milk
3 eggs
¼ teaspoon garlic powder
⅛ teaspoon ground nutmeg (optional)

Pinch of cayenne
½ pound sharp cheddar cheese, shredded
   (about 2 cups)
¼ pound Monterey Jack cheese, shredded
   (about 1 cup)
4 strips bacon, cooked until crisp and cut
   into ¼-inch pieces
1 cup frozen peas, thawed

Preheat the oven to 400°F and grease a 2-quart casserole dish.

Cook the pasta according to the package directions (leaving it al dente), drain, and set aside.

In a small bowl, combine the Parmesan cheese, bread crumbs, and butter.

In a large bowl, whisk together the evaporated milk, eggs, garlic powder, nutmeg, and cayenne.

Stir in the pasta, cheddar, Monterey Jack, bacon, and peas. Pour evenly into a casserole dish and sprinkle with the Parmesan cheese mixture. Bake uncovered for 30 to 40 minutes, until the edges are bubbly and the top is golden brown. Let rest for 10 minutes before serving.

# parmesan potato gnocchi with roasted garlic butter

## makes 4 to 6 servings

Finding good potato gnocchi has been a real challenge since we went gluten-free. Creating pasta from scratch, which makes it more authentic, turns out to be the best option. Serve this with the savory garlic butter or your own favorite sauce.

2 pounds russet potatoes (about 4)
½ cup potato starch, plus more for dusting
½ cup white rice flour
½ teaspoon salt
¼ teaspoon freshly ground white pepper
½ teaspoon baking powder

¼ cup finely grated Parmesan cheese, plus more for sprinkling
1 egg plus 1 egg white, beaten
Pinch of ground nutmeg (optional)
Roasted Garlic Butter (recipe follows)
1 tablespoon finely chopped fresh basil

Preheat the oven to 400°F.

Pierce the potatoes with a fork and bake for 1 hour.

In a small bowl, sift together the potato starch and white rice flour.

Peel the potatoes while they are still warm and pass through a potato ricer or shred them on a box grater into a large bowl. When the potatoes are cool, add the salt, white pepper, baking powder, ¼ cup of the Parmesan cheese, and beaten egg and egg white. Using your hands, mix the potatoes until moist. Add ½ cup of the flour mixture at a time while forming or kneading into a dough ball. Place the dough on a floured cutting board and cut into 6 pieces. Roll each piece into a rope about ½ inch in diameter and then cut into 1-inch pieces. Roll each piece down a gnocchi board or use the tines of a fork and press lightly on the dough to create ridges. Scatter

the gnocchi on a lightly floured baking sheet and continue until all are made.

Bring a large pot of salted water to a boil and place the gnocchi in the pot without overcrowding. Gnocchi are done about 90 seconds after they float to the surface. Remove the gnocchi with a skimmer or slotted spoon, toss them in a skillet over medium-high heat with the garlic butter, and cook for 3 to 4 minutes. Sprinkle with Parmesan cheese and fresh basil just before serving.

chef's note: If you are not cooking the gnocchi immediately, place them on a lightly floured sheet pan, wrap with plastic wrap, and refrigerate. Use them within one day.

To freeze the gnocchi, place them on a lightly floured sheet pan, wrap in plastic wrap, and place in the freezer until hardened. Transfer the gnocchi to tightly sealed individual freezer bags for storage. They will keep for up to 1 month.

# roasted garlic butter (makes about ½ cup)

**3 cloves garlic, peeled**
**1 teaspoon olive oil**
**8 tablespoons (1 stick) butter**
**Salt and freshly ground black pepper**

Preheat the oven to 300°F.

Place the garlic on a double layer of aluminum foil and drizzle with the olive oil. Fold the foil over the garlic into a sealed package and roast for 30 to 35 minutes. Place the roasted garlic on a cutting board and, using the flat side of a knife, press the garlic until a paste forms.

In a sauté pan over medium heat, melt the butter and whisk in the garlic. Bring to a simmer, and season to taste with salt and pepper.

# scallop and shrimp asiago risotto

## makes 4 to 6 servings

### cooking time: 45 to 50 minutes

This is a great dish to serve to guests on a special occasion because it looks fantastic. Bring a heaping bowl to the table and watch everyone dig in.

2½ cups gluten-free chicken broth
2 cups clam juice
2 tablespoons olive oil
2 tablespoons butter
1 cup finely chopped shallots or sweet onions
½ cup finely diced red bell pepper
2 cloves garlic, finely chopped
1½ cups Arborio rice

½ cup dry white wine
1 pound bay scallops
½ pound medium shrimp, peeled, deveined, and roughly chopped
⅓ cup shredded Asiago cheese
2 tablespoons finely chopped fresh flat-leaf parsley
Salt and freshly ground pepper

In a medium saucepan, bring the chicken broth and clam juice to a simmer.

In a large sauté pan over medium heat, heat the olive oil and butter. Add the shallots and red pepper and cook, stirring, for 4 to 5 minutes, until tender. Add the garlic and rice and cook, stirring, for 2 minutes. Add the wine, stirring constantly until the wine is absorbed by the rice. Ladle in ½ cup stock at a time, allowing the rice to absorb the liquid while stirring constantly before adding the next ½ cup. Continue cooking for a total of about 25 minutes, until the rice is creamy and tender. Stir the scallops and shrimp into the rice and continue cooking until the seafood is cooked, about 5 minutes.

Remove the risotto from the heat and stir in the Asiago cheese and parsley. Season with salt and pepper to taste.

# penne with bacon, arugula, white beans, and pecans

## makes 6 to 8 servings

Light and flavorful, this pasta's contrasting flavors and textures has moved family members to offer to pay me to make it again and again.

1 (12-ounce) package gluten-free penne or
  fusilli pasta
4 strips bacon, diced
4 cloves garlic, finely chopped
½ cup pecans, broken into pieces
10 ounces baby arugula

1 (15-ounce) can white cannellini beans,
  drained and rinsed
½ cup gluten-free chicken broth
3 tablespoons butter
½ cup finely grated Parmesan cheese
Salt and freshly ground black pepper

Cook the pasta according to the package directions, drain, and set aside. Place the pasta pot over medium heat and in it cook the bacon for 2 to 3 minutes, until it begins to crisp on the edges.

Add the garlic and pecans, cook for 1 minute, and then add the arugula, stirring until slightly wilted. Add the beans, pasta, chicken broth, and butter. Continue stirring until hot; then stir in the Parmesan cheese and season with salt and freshly ground pepper to taste. Serve immediately.

# pasta di san giuseppe

## makes 4 to 6 servings

St. Joseph's Day Noodles is a classic recipe from the Lucania region of Italy that is often served in Catholic homes on March 19th. The delicious combination of butter, walnuts, and Parmesan cheese slathered over fettuccine makes it a favorite in our home any night.

1 (12-ounce) package gluten-free
   fettuccine
5 cloves garlic
1 cup chopped walnuts, plus more for garnish
¼ cup gluten-free bread crumbs
¼ cup chopped fresh parsley
2 tablespoons gluten-free vegetable broth

¼ teaspoon salt
¼ cup olive oil
4 tablespoons (½ stick) butter
Finely grated Parmesan cheese, for
   sprinkling
1 tablespoon chopped fresh basil

Cook the pasta according to the package directions, drain, and set aside.

Place the garlic, 1 cup of the walnuts, the bread crumbs, parsley, vegetable broth and salt in a food processor and process while slowly drizzling in the olive oil until completely blended.

Melt the butter in a large sauté pan over medium-high heat, add the walnut mixture, and cook for 1 minute. Add the pasta and toss until hot and completely coated with sauce. Pour out into a large serving bowl and sprinkle with a generous amount of Parmesan cheese, the basil, and extra walnuts.

# pork and beef bolognese with tagliatelle

## makes 4 to 6 servings

Bolognese is a meat-based sauce that originated in Bologna, Italy. This is a quick meat sauce combination of pork and beef with tomatoes, fresh thyme, and red wine.

1 (12-ounce) package gluten-free
   tagliatelle or other wide pasta strands
3 tablespoons olive oil
1 cup chopped onion
2 tablespoons finely chopped garlic
1½ teaspoons chopped fresh thyme or
   ½ teaspoon dried
1 pound ground beef

1 pound ground pork
Salt and freshly ground black pepper
½ cup gluten-free beef broth
1½ cups canned crushed tomatoes
½ cup red wine
2 tablespoons chopped fresh parsley
1 cup shredded Parmesan cheese

Cook the tagliatelle according to the package directions, drain, and set aside.

In a large skillet over medium heat, heat the olive oil, add the onion, and cook, stirring, for about 2 minutes, until tender. Add the garlic and thyme and cook for about 1 minute. Raise the heat to medium-high and add the ground beef and pork, ¼ teaspoon salt, and ¼ teaspoon black pepper. Cook the meat for 6 to 7 minutes, breaking it up with a spoon. Add the beef broth and cook for 2 minutes. Then add the tomatoes and red wine, lower the heat, and simmer for 8 to 10 minutes. Remove from the heat and stir in the parsley and Parmesan cheese. Season with salt and pepper to taste and toss with the tagliatelle.

# battered and fried

When I was a young child, my parents owned a small cottage on Cape Cod. Summers were spent frolicking on the beach, searching for the perfect wave, and digging for clams. Vacation meals, at times, consisted of steamed or grilled seafood dishes and the occasional salad. However, more often than not, our beach dinners included giant platters of fried fish and chips, followed by huge bowls of frosty ice cream. Those lazy summer days instilled in me a genuine love for all seafood, with a special penchant for the fried fare, which still evokes a certain feeling of nostalgia whenever I sit down to eat it. I am often reminded of one place in particular, which was just a 5-minute bike ride from our cottage but one I would have walked to for miles in the pouring rain. This little "shack" was known for its huge, tasty platters of fried clams and hand-battered onion rings. It was always so fresh and crunchy, and tasted so good when smothered with creamy tartar sauce and a dollop of ketchup. Twenty-five years later, I wonder if that little landmark is still there today.

As I've traveled the country since the release of my first cookbook, I am surprised to learn how many people still look at fried food as a near delicacy and how much those on a gluten-free diet really miss it. Please understand that I am not advocating the consumption of fried foods on a daily basis, but rather everything in moderation. Fried items are a large part of the American food culture, and life without ever having a treat such as Crispy Fried Calamari with Easy Spicy Marinara or Crispy Chicken Fingers with Sweet-and-Sour Sauce is unimaginable. Recently, when I was invited to do a cooking demonstration in Fort Dodge, Iowa, a woman by the name of Meg asked me to come up with a gluten-free corn dog. We have quite a few country fairs here in Connecticut, and I have had my share of corn dogs, but I knew that for this woman from the corn capital of the world I would have to deliver a corn dog that would be the best of the best. I spent quite a few hours revising and revamping the recipe until it finally seemed right, and it ultimately passed the test of the Iowa corn dog connoisseurs. After that I thought, "Nothing can stop me now!" Mozzarella sticks, jalapeño poppers, fish and chips, calamari, and so much more fill this chapter. I hope these favorite fried treats put a smile on your face and stir a happy memory in your hearts!

# succulent fried scallops with tartar sauce

## makes 4 servings

A seashore staple can now easily be made at home and enjoyed year-round. Dip these in the special tartar sauce and there will be no leftovers.

¼ cup white rice flour
¼ cup cornstarch
½ teaspoon paprika
½ teaspoon salt
1 egg

1 tablespoon buttermilk
½ cup gluten-free bread crumbs
1 pound bay scallops
Vegetable oil, for deep frying
Tartar Sauce (recipe follows)

In a medium bowl, whisk together the white rice flour, cornstarch, paprika, and salt.

In a second bowl, beat together the egg and buttermilk.

Place the bread crumbs in a third bowl.

Dry the scallops with paper towels and dip them into the flour mixture, shaking off the excess. Dip them into the egg mixture and then the bread crumbs.

In a large, heavy saucepan or Dutch oven, heat 3 inches of vegetable oil until a deep-fat thermometer reads 360°F. Add the scallops a handful at a time without crowding the pan and fry for 1 to 2 minutes, until golden brown. Drain on paper towels and serve with tartar sauce.

# tartar sauce (makes 1¼ cups)

¾ cup mayonnaise
¼ cup finely chopped dill pickle
2 tablespoons finely chopped green onion
1 tablespoon drained capers

1 tablespoon freshly squeezed lemon juice
½ teaspoon gluten-free Worcestershire
   sauce
¼ teaspoon hot sauce

In a medium bowl, whisk together all the ingredients. Cover and refrigerate for up to 2 weeks.

# crispy fried calamari

## makes 4 to 6 servings

Our dear friends Patty and Dennis and their four children—Jacob, Sarah, James, and Joel—celebrated New Year's Eve with us. I set them up with a taste testing experiment using blindfolds and three types of fried calamari. Dennis is a certified calamari connoisseur, and he picked this clear winner for us.

1 cup corn flour
¼ cup white rice flour
¾ teaspoon salt, plus more for sprinkling
1 egg
1 cup evaporated milk

Vegetable oil, for deep frying
1 pound squid with tentacles, cleaned and cut into ½-inch rings
1 lemon, cut into wedges
1 cup Easy Spicy Marinara (page 125)

In a medium bowl, sift together the corn flour, white rice flour, and ¾ teaspoon salt.

In a separate bowl, whisk together the egg and evaporated milk until frothy.

Heat 3 to 4 inches of oil in a large heavy saucepan over medium-high heat until a deep-fat thermometer reads 360°F. Working in small batches, dip the squid into the milk mixture and then toss in the flour mixture until coated.

Drop the squid into the hot oil in batches, without crowding, and fry for 30 to 40 seconds, until golden brown. Using tongs, transfer the squid to paper towels to drain. Place the squid on a platter, sprinkle with salt, and serve with lemon wedges and spicy marinara.

# corn dogs

## makes 6

This recipe was developed to appease the crowd of wonderful people I met during my talk and demo at the Celiac Sprue Association Conference in Fort Dodge, Iowa. I knew this one was a winner when it pleased the leading corn dog enthusiasts in America! I enjoy my corn dogs served with spicy mustard.

Vegetable oil, for deep frying
½ cup cornmeal
½ cup white rice flour
1 teaspoon kosher salt
½ teaspoon baking powder
¼ teaspoon baking soda
¼ teaspoon dry mustard

¼ teaspoon cayenne
½ cup canned cream-style corn
½ cup buttermilk
1 egg, beaten
2 tablespoons finely minced onion
2 tablespoons cornstarch
6 hot dogs

Pour 4 inches of oil into a large pot and heat until a deep-fat thermometer reads 360°F. In a medium bowl, whisk together the cornmeal, white rice flour, salt, baking powder, baking soda, dry mustard, and cayenne.

In a separate bowl, whisk together the canned corn, buttermilk, egg, and onion. Blend the dry ingredients into the wet ingredients and mix until the batter is just blended. Allow the batter to rest for 10 to 15 minutes before using.

Place the cornstarch in a shallow pan and pour the batter into a tall water glass until it is three-quarters full. Slide a skewer into one end of each hot dog, making a handle for dipping it in the batter. Roll the hot dog in cornstarch until coated and then shake off the excess. Dip the hot dog in and out of the batter in the glass and then slowly lower the coated hot dog into the hot oil while gently and carefully releasing it from the skewer. Cook a few at a time for 3 to 4 minutes, until golden brown. Remove with tongs and allow to drain on a rack or paper towel before eating. Serve drizzled with the desired condiments.

# fried mozzarella sticks with easy spicy marinara

## makes 4 to 6 servings

I've heard other chefs proclaim that you haven't tried great fried mozzarella sticks until you've made them at home. But for someone with celiac disease, finding a coating that will remain golden brown and still hold in all the gooey, melted mozzarella is easier said than done. When my three-year-old exclaimed, "These are AMAZING!" I knew we had gotten it right!

¼ cup white rice flour
2 tablespoons cornstarch
¾ cup gluten-free bread crumbs
¼ cup finely grated Parmesan cheese
1 tablespoon finely chopped fresh parsley
½ teaspoon garlic powder
¼ teaspoon dried oregano

⅛ teaspoon freshly ground black pepper
2 eggs
¼ cup milk
Vegetable oil, for deep frying
1 (16-ounce) package mozzarella cheese, cut into 16 sticks
Easy Spicy Marinara (recipe follows)

In a small bowl, whisk together the white rice flour and cornstarch.

In a medium bowl, whisk together the bread crumbs, Parmesan cheese, parsley, garlic powder, oregano, and pepper.

In a third bowl, beat together the eggs and milk.

Fill a medium saucepan halfway with vegetable oil and heat over medium-high heat until a deep-fat thermometer reads 360°F.

Dredge the mozzarella sticks in the flour mixture until completely coated, dip into the egg mixture, and then coat thoroughly with the bread crumb mixture.

Fry the mozzarella sticks a few at a time in the hot oil for 20 to 30 seconds, until golden brown. Drain on paper towels and then serve with the marinara sauce.

# easy spicy marinara (makes 1 cup)

**1 cup favorite gluten-free marinara**
**⅛ to ¼ teaspoon hot red pepper flakes**
**1 clove garlic, minced**

In a small saucepan, combine the marinara, red pepper flakes, and garlic. Bring to a simmer and pour into a serving bowl.

# fish and chips

## makes 4 to 6 servings

Often sorely missed by the gluten-free population, this recipe succeeds in bringing back an angler's favorite—tender batter-dipped fish and chips, cooked to golden perfection and topped with a tartar sauce . . . yum!

Vegetable oil, for deep frying
5 Yukon Gold potatoes (about 1½ pounds)
1 cup white rice flour
1 tablespoon baking powder
1 teaspoon kosher salt, plus more for sprinkling
¼ teaspoon Old Bay Seasoning

⅛ teaspoon cayenne
2 egg yolks
¾ cup gluten-free beer (such as Bard's Tale) or soda water
1 pound tilapia, cod, or pollack fillets
½ cup cornstarch
Tartar Sauce (page 121)

In a large saucepan, heat 3 inches of oil over medium-high heat until it reads 320°F on a deep-fat thermometer.

Cut the potatoes into ⅛-inch slices and fry, parcooking the chips for 2 to 3 minutes. Place on paper towels to cool completely. Increase the temperature of the oil to 350°F and fry the chips a second time for 2 to 3 minutes, until golden brown.

In a medium bowl, mix together the white rice flour, baking powder, 1 teaspoon of the kosher salt, the Old Bay Seasoning, and the cayenne. Add the egg yolks and beer and whisk until a smooth batter forms. Set aside.

Pat the fish fillets dry with paper towels and cut into ½-inch strips. Dredge the fish strips in the cornstarch and dip into the beer batter. Allow the excess batter to drip off and lower into the hot oil. Cook the fish for 3 to 4 minutes, until golden brown, and serve with tartar sauce.

# jalapeño poppers

## makes 4 servings

A blend of sharp yellow cheddar, Monterey Jack, and cream cheeses makes up the rich, delicious filling for these spicy jalapeño snack bites. Prepare them by the dozen, as they will disappear quickly after emerging from the deep fryer!

12 jalapeño peppers
¼ cup shredded Monterey Jack cheese (about 2 ounces)
¼ cup shredded sharp yellow cheddar (about 2 ounces)
½ cup softened cream cheese or goat cheese
¼ cup salsa or pico de gallo
2 eggs
1 cup gluten-free bread crumbs
2 teaspoons dried oregano
Vegetable oil, for deep frying

Place the jalapeños in a pot of boiling water, boil for 5 minutes, drain, and cool to room temperature.

In a medium bowl, stir together the Monterey Jack cheese, cheddar, cream cheese, and salsa. Cut slits down one side of each pepper (leaving the stem) and, using the tip of a knife, remove the seeds and membranes. Using a small spoon, fill the jalapeños with the cheese mixture and then press the seams together to return the jalapeños to their original shape. In a small bowl, beat the eggs until frothy.

In a medium bowl, whisk together the bread crumbs and oregano.

In a large heavy sauté pan or Dutch oven, heat 3 inches of oil over medium-high heat until a deep-fat thermometer reads 350°F. One at a time, dip a jalapeño into the egg, allow the excess to drip off, and then roll in the bread crumb mixture. Repeat again, dipping into the egg mixture and then into the bread crumbs, forming a second layer.

Slowly place a few jalapeños at a time in the oil and fry for 1 to 2 minutes, until golden brown. Drain on paper towels before serving.

# crispy chicken fingers with sweet-and-sour sauce

## makes 4 to 6 servings

My father-in-law, Ed, is a giant fan of the sweet-and-sour chicken at our local Chinese restaurant. I recently made a batch of these chicken strips for him and my two young sons to enjoy for dinner. Ed dipped into the sweet-and-sour sauce, Joseph had honey mustard, and Andrew needed only ketchup. Everyone was happy and satisfied!

1½ cups white rice flour
½ teaspoon paprika
2 cups soda water
1½ pounds boneless, skinless chicken, cut into 3-inch-long by ½-inch-wide strips

Vegetable oil, for deep frying
Salt
Sweet-and-Sour Sauce (recipe follows)

In a medium bowl, whisk together the white rice flour and paprika. Slowly whisk in the soda water until the mixture has the consistency of pancake batter. In a large heavy sauté pan or Dutch oven over medium-high heat, heat 3 inches of oil until a deep-fat thermometer reads 360°F. Dip the chicken strips into the batter and then slowly drop a few at a time into the hot oil. Cook for 4 to 5 minutes, until golden brown, and then place on paper towels to drain, sprinkling with a touch of salt. Continue with the remaining chicken strips until all are cooked. Serve with a bowl of sweet-and-sour sauce or your favorite dipping sauce.

## sweet-and-sour sauce (makes about 1 cup)

2 teaspoons cornstarch
1 tablespoon water
¼ cup rice wine vinegar
¼ cup packed brown sugar

¼ cup canned crushed pineapple, drained
1 tablespoon ketchup
1 teaspoon gluten-free soy sauce
⅛ teaspoon ground ginger

In a small bowl, blend together the cornstarch and water until a smooth paste forms. Set aside.

In a medium saucepan over medium-high heat, whisk together the vinegar, brown sugar, pineapple, ketchup, soy sauce, and ginger. Bring to a boil and then whisk in the cornstarch mixture. Boil until the sauce thickens and then remove from the heat. Place in a blender or food processor and blend until smooth. Serve hot or at room temperature.

# chapter 8

# manna (breads and biscuits)

The gluten-free revolution began decades ago, with the primary focus on baking and making breads. This is not at all surprising, as for many years persons with celiac disease couldn't find even a decent slice of bread to make a sandwich or anything that resembled a real bagel, English muffin, or hot dog roll. Fortunately for all of us in the industry, times have changed quite a bit. These days most health food stores, buying co-ops, and even mainstream supermarkets are carrying quality brands of gluten-free breads, muffins, and bagels that actually taste like their wheat-laden counterparts. They have an improved taste and texture and are even becoming more affordable. While the market is on the upswing, there are still products that are missing or just don't measure up to the real stuff.

Before my wife was diagnosed with celiac disease, we used to visit a small Italian restaurant in rural Connecticut. The owner would come to the table wearing his funny little cap and sharing stories about the Old Country. One of the items we both loved was the rosemary garlic baguette served with extra-virgin olive oil and black pepper. This was the type of bread my wife still sorely missed, and that inspired me to re-create these baguettes, slightly crusty on the outside and soft and chewy on the inside.

Another recipe in this chapter on manna is my aunt Rosemary's Pepperoni-Pesto Cheese Wheels—a mainstay appetizer presented during her famous Thanksgiving dinners on Long Island. The combination of spicy pepperoni and melted imported mozzarella cheese rolled up and baked in gluten-free bread dough is sure to please everyone at your table. I've also included a recipe for the newest trend on the barbecue—grilled pizza. If you have never experienced a gentle, smoky flavor and a crispy, crunchy sensation when biting into gluten-free pizza crust, you must try this. It will remind you of those delicious restaurant-made thin-crust pizzas baked to perfection in a wood-fired oven.

For those with a sweet tooth, there is a quick version of that old childhood classic, monkey bread. Swimming in butterscotch and pecans (and minus the monkeys), this special bread treat is great for breakfast or dessert. And those in search of a high- protein, high-fiber bread must try the Molasses Flax Sandwich Bread. I hope these recipes will surprise and delight everyone in your home and make believers out of everyone who thinks great gluten-free bread "just can't be done."

# molasses flax sandwich bread

makes one 9 by 5-inch loaf

rising time: 1 to 1½ hours

baking time: 20 to 25 minutes

This is an extremely hearty and versatile dark bread with flavorful contrasts of sweet molasses and nutty flaxseeds. Creating it was a labor of love, requiring multiple revisions until finally it resembled the hearty brown bread my aunt Doris used to serve with her baked beans on Sunday afternoons. It's a high-protein, high-fiber bread that toasts beautifully for breakfast, makes awesome turkey sandwiches for lunch, and can be torn and smothered with butter at the dinner table.

1 cup warm water (105° to 110°F)
½ cup warm milk (105° to 110°F)
1 tablespoon active dry yeast
3 cups Montina All-Purpose Baking Flour Blend
½ cup gluten-free oats
¼ cup flaxseed meal

1 tablespoon xanthan gum
1½ teaspoons salt
½ teaspoon baking soda
½ cup molasses
4 tablespoons (½ stick) butter, melted
1 teaspoon apple cider vinegar
3 eggs, separated

In a small bowl, whisk together the warm water and milk and sprinkle the yeast on top. Set aside.

Using an electric mixer, mix together the Montina flour blend, oats, flaxseed meal, xanthan gum, salt, and baking soda. With the mixer running on low speed, add the molasses, melted butter, vinegar, egg yolks, and yeast mixture. Increase the mixer to high and beat for 1 to 2 minutes, until incorporated.

In a separate bowl with clean beaters, beat the egg whites until soft peaks form—the beaten whites should look similar to whipped cream. Fold the egg whites into the batter and cover with plastic wrap. Allow the dough to rise in a warm area for 1 hour.

Beat the mixture on high for 2 minutes. Pour the batter evenly into a greased loaf pan, cover loosely with plastic wrap, and allow to rise for 1 to 1½ hours, until the batter is slightly above the pan.

Preheat the oven to 375°F and bake the bread for 20 minutes. Cover the pan with aluminum foil and bake for another 20 to 25 minutes. Remove the bread from the baking pan and allow to cool on a rack.

# jalapeño-cheddar buttermilk biscuits

## makes 1 dozen

Ah, biscuits . . . an old southern cooking jewel and the perfect complement for fried chicken. I have yet to meet the person who turns down a good biscuit, and I have finally got the recipe down for a great jalapeño-cheddar version. Serve them warm with butter for breakfast or a snack, alongside the Mexican meal of your choice, or dip them into gravy!

1 cup tapioca flour
½ cup sweet sorghum flour
½ cup white rice flour
½ cup cornstarch
½ cup potato starch
1 tablespoon xanthan gum
1 tablespoon baking powder
1½ teaspoons baking soda

1 teaspoon salt
½ teaspoon sugar
¼ cup vegetable shortening
4 tablespoons (½ stick) unsalted butter, diced
½ pound shredded sharp cheddar cheese
2 jalapeños, seeded and minced
1½ cups buttermilk

Preheat the oven to 425°F and grease a baking sheet.

In a medium bowl, whisk together the tapioca flour, sorghum flour, white rice flour, cornstarch, potato starch, xanthan gum, baking powder, baking soda, salt, and sugar. Using your fingers or a pastry blender, rub or cut the shortening and butter into the dry ingredients until the mixture is coarse and crumbly. Stir in the cheddar cheese and jalapeños and then add the buttermilk, stirring until the ingredients are thoroughly mixed.

Scoop out ¼ cup of dough, shape into a 1-inch-thick round, and place on the greased pan. Repeat with the rest of the dough, leaving 2 inches of space between the biscuits. Bake for 15 minutes or until golden brown. Remove from the oven and let cool on wire racks before serving.

# grilled pizza crust

## makes 4 (6-inch) pizza crusts

### rising time: 1 hour

One of the hottest new trends in grilling or barbecue is the grilled pizza. Start with the perfect crust and top it with your favorite sauce, vegetables, meats, and cheeses. Then place it on a hot grill and allow it to cook to crunchy perfection.

¾ cup warm water
1 tablespoon sugar
1 tablespoon quick-rising dry yeast
1½ cups tapioca flour, plus more for dusting
1¼ cups brown rice flour
¼ cup whole ground flaxseed meal
¼ cup potato starch

1 tablespoon xanthan gum
1 teaspoon garlic powder
½ teaspoon salt
2 tablespoons milk
2 tablespoons extra-virgin olive oil, plus more for grilling
1 egg, beaten
1 tablespoon Italian seasoning

In a small bowl, combine the warm water, sugar, and yeast.

Using a food processor, pulse together the tapioca flour, brown rice flour, flaxseed meal, potato starch, xanthan gum, garlic powder, and salt. Add the milk, olive oil, egg, yeast mixture, and Italian seasoning, pulsing until the mixture begins to form a dough ball.

Remove the dough from the bowl and place on a lightly (tapioca) floured cutting board. Divide the dough into quarters and form into dough balls. Cover the dough balls with a clean towel and let them rest in a warm place for 1 hour, allowing the dough to rise slightly.

Lightly flour a cutting board with tapioca flour and roll out the dough into 6-inch rounds. Using your fingers, pinch the sides of the dough to form an edge. The crust is now ready to grill.

chef's note: To grill the pizzas, preheat a grill to medium-high heat and oil the grates. Using a spatula, slide the prepared pizza crust off the cutting board onto the hot grates, shut the lid, and cook for 4 to 5 minutes, until the bottom is golden brown. Brush the top side with oil, then flip the crust over and top with the desired toppings. Good combinations include pizza sauce and mozzarella cheese; barbecue sauce, shredded cooked chicken, and cheddar cheese; and pesto and mozzarella cheese. Shut the lid and cook for 4 to 5 minutes longer, until the bottom crust is crispy and the toppings are melted and hot.

To bake the pizza, place the rolled-out dough on a greased baking sheet, top with the ingredients, and bake in a preheated 450°F oven for 12 to 15 minutes, until the edges are golden and the cheese is melted.

# rosemary garlic baguettes

## makes 2 loaves

### rising time: 1½ hours

### baking time: 35 to 40 minutes

This is a huge craving that my wife had—the crunchy-on-the-outside, chewy-and-garlicky-on-the-inside, hot, crusty baguette. Whether served with pasta dishes or alone, slathered in butter, olive oil, or cream cheese, this one is sure to please.

¼ cup extra-virgin olive oil
2 tablespoons apple cider vinegar
2 eggs, separated, plus 1 egg white
1¼ cups warm water (110°F)
3 tablespoons sugar
2 tablespoons active dry yeast
1¼ cups tapioca starch, plus more for dusting
¾ cup white rice flour
½ cup brown rice flour

½ cup sorghum flour
¼ cup flaxseed meal
¼ cup corn flour
1 tablespoon xanthan gum
½ teaspoon salt
¼ teaspoon freshly ground black pepper
3 cloves garlic, peeled and minced
1 tablespoon minced fresh rosemary
2 teaspoons sesame seeds
½ teaspoon kosher salt

In a medium bowl, whisk together the olive oil, vinegar, and 2 egg yolks; set aside. Place 2 of the egg whites in a bowl and beat until light and frothy. Set aside.

In a separate bowl, combine the warm water, sugar, and yeast; set aside.

Using an electric mixer with a paddle on low to medium speed, combine the tapioca starch, white rice flour, brown rice flour, sorghum flour, flaxseed meal, corn flour, xanthan gum, salt, and pepper. Add the egg yolk mixture, yeast mixture, and the garlic and rosemary, blending until the mixture pulls together and forms a moist dough. Add the beaten egg whites and mix until incorporated. Transfer the dough to a cutting board dusted with tapioca flour and cut into two equal pieces.

On the greased pan, shape the dough into two 16-inch-long by 2-inch-wide baguettes. (The dough will be sticky, so have a bowl of tapioca flour available to dip your hands.) Cover the loaves with a clean dish towel or plastic wrap and allow to rise in a warm area for 1½ hours.

Preheat the oven to 375°F. In a small bowl, whisk the remaining egg white. Using a brush, paint each baguette with egg white and sprinkle evenly with sesame seeds and kosher salt. Using a razor blade or sharp knife, make 8 slashes across the top of each baguette, about 2 inches apart and ¼ inch deep. Bake 30 to 35 minutes, until golden brown. Serve with a bowl of olive oil with crushed black pepper or softened butter.

# pepperoni-pesto cheese wheels

## makes 12 wheels

## rising time: 1½ hours

## baking time: 15 to 20 minutes

My aunt Rosemary typically served pepperoni cheese bread at the start of her eight-course Thanksgiving dinner. With a few changes, now everyone can enjoy a gluten-free version.

¾ cup warm water (110°F)
1 tablespoon sugar
1 tablespoon active dry yeast
1 cup tapioca flour, plus more for dusting
½ cup sorghum flour
½ cup brown rice flour
½ cup white rice flour
¼ cup potato starch
¼ cup cornstarch

¼ cup flaxseed meal
2 teaspoons xanthan gum
1 teaspoon garlic powder
¼ teaspoon salt
2 tablespoons milk
2 tablespoons extra-virgin olive oil
⅓ cup pesto
¼ pound pepperoni (about 60 thin slices)
1 cup shredded mozzarella

In a small bowl, mix the water, sugar, and yeast. Set aside.

Using a food processor, blend the tapioca flour, sorghum flour, brown rice flour, white rice flour, potato starch, cornstarch, flaxseed meal, xanthan gum, garlic powder, and salt. Add the milk and olive oil and blend until just combined. Slowly drizzle in the yeast mixture, blending until thoroughly combined.

Transfer the dough to a cutting board, cover with a dish towel, and allow to rise in a warm place for 30 minutes. Grease a 12-cup muffin tin and set aside.

When the dough has risen, dust a sheet of wax paper with tapioca flour and place the dough on top. Sprinkle the top of the dough with more tapioca flour and place another sheet on top. Roll out into a 15 by 10-inch rectangle. Remove the top sheet of wax paper and coat the entire surface with a thin layer of pesto, followed by pepperoni slices, then mozzarella cheese. Then, using the bottom piece of wax paper on the 15-inch side, slowly roll the dough away from you into the shape of a log or jelly roll, pinching the seam together. (It is important to roll slowly with one hand while using the other to assist in peeling the dough away from the wax paper, which may stick.) Using a sharp knife, cut 12 even slices about 1 inch thick, and place them cut side down in the muffin cups. Cover with a clean dish towel, place in a warm area, and allow to rise for 1 hour. Preheat the oven to 375°F and bake until golden brown, 15 to 20 minutes.

# quick and easy monkey bread

makes 1 round tube pan

rising time: 6 to 12 hours

baking time: 30 to 35 minutes

½ cup buttermilk
¼ cup apple cider or juice
¼ cup granulated sugar
1 tablespoon active dry yeast
1¼ cups tapioca flour, plus ¼ cup for
    dusting
1 cup brown rice flour
¼ cup potato starch
¼ cup flaxseed meal
2½ teaspoons xanthan gum
2 teaspoons baking powder
½ teaspoon salt

¼ teaspoon baking soda
¼ teaspoon plus ⅛ teaspoon ground
    cinnamon
8 tablespoons (1 stick) butter,
    plus 2 tablespoons melted
2 tablespoons vegetable oil
1 egg plus 1 egg white
1 teaspoon vanilla extract
½ cup chopped pecans
1 cup packed brown sugar
1 (3.4-ounce) box instant butterscotch
    pudding

In a small saucepan or microwave-safe bowl, whisk together the buttermilk and apple cider. Warm to 110°F, add the sugar, and sprinkle the yeast on top. Set aside.

In a large bowl, whisk together 1¼ cups of the tapioca flour, the brown rice flour, potato starch, flaxseed meal, xanthan gum, baking powder, salt, baking soda, and ¼ teaspoon of the cinnamon. Stir in the 2 tablespoons of melted butter, oil, egg, egg white, vanilla, and yeast mixture and mix until thoroughly combined. The dough will be sticky. Leave the dough in the mixing bowl, cover with plastic wrap, place in a warm spot, and allow to rest for 20 minutes.

Generously grease a 10-inch Bundt pan. Sprinkle the pecans in the bottom. In a small saucepan over medium heat, melt the brown sugar, remaining 8 tablespoons butter, and remaining ⅛ teaspoon cinnamon. Set aside. Have the remaining ¼ cup of tapioca flour on hand for dusting. Using a small ice cream scoop, scoop dough from the bowl and roll it into golf ball–size balls between floured hands. Drop each into the pan. Sprinkle the pudding mix evenly over the dough balls, then pour the brown sugar and butter mixture over the top. Cover with plastic wrap and refrigerate for 6 to 12 hours. Remove from the refrigerator, uncover, and place in a warm area for 1 hour.

Preheat the oven to 350°F and bake for 30 to 35 minutes, until golden brown. Remove from the oven, invert onto a large serving plate, and cool for 15 minutes before serving.

# sweet treats

In Chapter 7, I wrote about the shore house where my sister, Dana, and I spent many a summer, breathing in the salt air and enjoying the carefree summer days of youth. Those memories bring to mind another food experience that was both charming and unique. Every warm and sunny morning there was a little old man who would wind through the cottage communities in his green 1940s Ford pickup. Stocked in the back and ready for sale were pans of freshly baked goods that he and his wife had toiled over the night before. He invariably had available an assortment of pies, cakes, cookies, and brownies, including his locally famous signature item—old-fashioned molasses cookies. These were as good as any gramma could make, with the perfect balance of molasses and brown sugar, chewy and delicious and dusted with white granulated sugar. This chapter was written to include such favorites as these and to share recipes for a variety of gluten-free desserts to fulfill all our cravings and satiate that sweet tooth.

If you were to ask my son Joseph what his favorite part of any meal is, he would answer with one resounding word: DESSERT! And perhaps he is not the only one, as is confirmed when you watch eyes light up when a dessert menu is passed around. For me, the perfect dessert is a classic, but never boring, pie. For so many people who are baking gluten-free, this dessert has become a colossal challenge. Thus, this chapter contains a much-requested pie crust tutorial that covers a variety of different crusts and takes the guesswork and frustration out of assembling the perfect pie. After you read this chapter, your Down East Blueberry Pie will bake to perfection in a sugar and oats pie crust, while Aunt Lil's Creamy Cheesecake will sit atop a sweet, buttery Vanilla Cookie Crumb Pie Crust bottom. My traditional Buttery Flaky Pie Crust will encompass an Mississippi Sweet Potato Pie filling fit for a king. All three are to die for, yet completely unique with regard to ingredients, preparation, cooking time, and final taste and texture.

Gluten-free versions of those Old-Fashioned Molasses Cookies are joined by Butterscotch Apple Cookies, Chocolate-Espresso Cookies by Emily, and that old holiday favorite for which I am proud to offer a gluten-free alternative, Russian Teacakes. I have also included recipes that will shake up the usual brownie fare and take the chocolate treat to a whole new level. All are tasty, and some are even nutritious and packed with protein and fiber, such as Bittersweet Bean Brownies. When you are feeling adventurous (or like you need a stiff drink!), try the Bard's Gold Beer Brownies. Whatever version you choose, you are sure to say, "Oh, these are soooooo good!"

# pie crust tutorial

Making a pie crust for the first time can be an intimidating experience, even for the well-seasoned chef. However, by knowing a few secrets and following the right directions, anyone can easily become a pastry crust expert.

Right away, most bakers will notice a significant difference in texture between a gluten-free pie crust and a wheat-based pie crust. When a wheat-based dough is kneaded into a ball, it naturally becomes stiff as the gluten proteins are activated. Gluten-free pie dough is missing that activation, forcing the baker to give up the "kneading" technique and to use more of a "cupping" procedure, similar to that used in forming a snowball.

For my gluten-free recipes, work the dough just long enough to incorporate the butter and shortening evenly, while packing or forming it into a tightened ball. Next, wrap the dough ball tightly in plastic wrap to help it hold its shape while it is refrigerated. Refrigerating wheat-based pie crusts allows the gluten to "rest." Refrigeration for a gluten-free pie crust also allows the dough to rest, but primarily so that the dough will become easier to roll and form properly in the pie plate.

## choosing the ingredients

In making the perfect pie crust, the first things to consider are the ingredients. What exactly is it that makes a pie crust really good? Pie tasters extraordinaire always focus on two important factors: Is the crust flaky, and is the crust buttery? Putting all health consciousness aside, there is no way around it—perfect flakiness comes from vegetable shortening or lard, and melt-in-your-mouth flavor comes from real butter. Using a combination of the two makes the perfect pastry crust for any pie. The other ingredients needed include a simple blend of white rice flour, tapioca flour, sugar, baking soda, xanthan gum, and salt. Although there is nothing wrong with using a food processor, I prefer to make my crusts the good old-fashioned way—by hand. The following are instructions that will assist you when preparing a single- or double-crust recipe for pie crusts.

## cutting in the shortening and butter

Once the dry ingredients are mixed together, the next step is to cut in the shortening and butter. This is done to reduce the larger pieces of fat to smaller pieces, while incorporating them into the dry ingredients. These small pieces of butter and shortening are what melt or break down during the baking process, imparting a delicious flavor and proper texture to the crust. This is easily accomplished by using your choice of a standard pastry cutter, two butter knives, or, my preferred method, your hands. If using your hands, try squeezing the shortening between your fingers to break the fat down into peanut-size pieces.

## adding the liquids

At this point, you will add your liquid and combine the wet and dry ingredients until a dough ball forms. Many people use water to bind together a pie crust, but I have found that using milk imparts a richer, smoother flavor that makes a much better-tasting pie. Adding the milk a small amount at a time helps to keep the consistency just right, so that you don't end up with a wet, unworkable dough ball. A dough ball that is slightly tacky and not too wet is much easier to roll out and shape in the pan. After the ball is formed, wrap it in plastic wrap and refrigerate the dough overnight.

## rolling and forming the dough

Start with a clean and clear work area, such as a countertop or a large cutting board that allows you room to roll out the dough. Begin by taking a piece of wax paper, slightly larger than 12 inches long, and lay it flat on the work surface. Place the refrigerated pastry dough on the wax paper and use your hands to press firmly on the dough to flatten it out slightly. Next, take another sheet of wax paper, lay it flat on top of the pastry dough, and use a rolling pin to roll out the dough. The trick to rolling pastry dough is to begin in the middle of the dough and roll toward the outer edges. Apply just enough pressure on the rolling pin to make the edges the same thickness as the middle. The goal is to roll out the dough, as close as you can, to a 12-inch circle.

## panning the dough

Transferring a gluten-free pie dough from the cutting board to the pan has always been a challenge for the gluten-free baker. Many have found that the dough cracks and breaks easily, leaving holes and gaps that need to be patched back together. Keep in mind that regular pastry crust dough contains the strong, elastic gluten that assists in holding the dough together and keeps it pliable as it is moved from working surface to pan. When working with gluten-free flours, additional measures must be taken to make the panning process a success.

The key here is to use wax paper as described and to have a very heavily greased pan ready for the pastry dough transfer. Begin by removing the wax paper from the top of the pastry dough. Gently slide one hand under the wax paper underneath the dough, supporting it slightly with your fingers. Next, using your other hand, place the opening of the pie pan on top of the dough. Holding your hands as steady as possible, quickly invert the dough into the pan so that the wax paper ends up on top, with the dough inside the pan.

Place the pan back on your work surface and use your fingers to press the dough into the bottom of the pan. Carefully peel off the wax paper that is now on top of the dough. There will be an overhang of dough, some of which may break during this step but can easily be patched later. If you are making a single pie crust, use a paring knife and trim the dough, leaving a 1-inch overhang of excess dough. Then, using your fingers, begin rolling the excess overhang toward the pie plate rim. Once the entire edge is covered, use your fingers and firmly pinch the dough around the entire pan. If you prefer, you can use a fork to press the tines against the dough, working your way around the edge. Some people prefer to cut this excess dough off, but leaving it on will make a thick, tasty edge around the whole pie.

## prebaking (blind baking) a single pastry crust

In the following recipes, several of the pies require a prebaked pie crust. When prebaking a pie crust, some pastry chefs recommend weighting the dough with pie weights or beans to prevent it from puffing up and cracking. Although this works for some, I prefer a no-weights method. Simply take a paring knife and use the tip to make a couple of pinholes in the bottom of the pastry dough before baking. The holes will bake shut, the dough will puff up ever so slightly, and the bottom will not crack. I find that forgoing the weights in the middle of the pie leaves a lighter, flakier pie crust.

If you do choose the weighting-down method, try using beans instead of weights. Cut a piece of aluminum foil or parchment paper just slightly larger than the center circle of the pie pan. Lay it on the dough and fill it with a single layer of dried beans. This will keep your dough from puffing up and give you a stiffer, denser bottom crust.

## making a double pie crust

The recipe for a double pie crust makes enough for two dough balls. The first ball is for the bottom crust, and the second is for the top. You will use the same method that you used to roll out the single pie crust, using the wax paper. The difference is to roll the top crust dough just big enough to cover your filling and to leave a slight overhang on the edge of the pan. You also want to use a pastry brush and a little milk, water, or egg wash to moisten the edges of the bottom crust. This will act as an adhesive when the top crust is attached.

After rolling the dough to the desired-size circle, peel the wax paper off the top of the pastry dough, grip the bottom of the wax paper closest to you, and flip it over while placing it on top of the filling. Slowly remove the wax paper from the top of the crust. Next, trim the excess dough from the edges, leaving about a $\frac{1}{2}$-inch overhang. Using your fingers, pinch the bottom and top crusts together, working your way around the entire edge of the pie pan. If you prefer using the fork method, trim the dough along the edge of the pan and then use the tines of the fork to seal the bottom and top crusts together. At this point, use a paring knife to cut four to six small holes in the top crust, which will allow the steam to escape during baking so the pie crust doesn't crack.

## baking the pie

Always have a thermometer in your oven to confirm that the desired temperature is being maintained. If the temperature is too high, you will end up with a dark brown outer crust and an uncooked center. If the temperature is too low, you will have a pale, unattractive crust that isn't as flaky as you desired. I recommend baking all pies in the center of the oven, with a large cookie sheet underneath to catch any drippings that may escape. This keeps the oven clean and the kitchen free from filling up with unwanted smoke. Check the pie halfway through the baking process. If it looks like one side is slightly darker than the other, turn or rotate the pie so that it browns evenly. If your pie edges brown too fast, use a piece of aluminum foil to cover the area.

## cooling the pie

It is very important to allow the pie to cool completely before cutting and serving. This cooling time allows the filling to firm up and the ingredients to reach their desired flavor. If a fruit or custard pie is cut while still hot, the filling will leak out all over the pie plate. Practicing patience during this last step in the pie baking process will make you a much happier pie baker.

# buttery flaky pie crust

## makes 1 (9-inch) pie

You will find that this pie has all the qualities needed to complement many of your favorite pie fillings. Butter gives this crust great flavor, while shortening gives it flakiness.

1¼ cups white rice flour
1 cup tapioca flour
1 tablespoon sugar
½ teaspoon baking soda
½ teaspoon xanthan gum

½ teaspoon salt
¼ teaspoon ground cinnamon
½ cup vegetable shortening
4 tablespoons (½ stick) butter, cold
½ cup milk

In a medium bowl, whisk together the white rice flour, tapioca flour, sugar, baking soda, xanthan gum, salt, and cinnamon. Add the shortening and butter. Using your fingertips, a pastry blender, or two butter knives, rub or cut the shortening and butter into the dry ingredients until it forms the texture of a coarse meal, with pea-size pieces. Use a fork to gradually stir in the milk to moisten the dry ingredients. Using your hands, form the dough into a ball and wrap in plastic wrap. Refrigerate for at least 2 hours or up to 1 week.

Preheat the oven to 350°F. Butter a 9-inch pie plate and set it aside.

Roll the dough between two pieces of wax paper into a 12-inch round. Remove the wax paper from the top of the round and invert the pie plate on top of the dough. Place your other hand under the wax paper and turn the round over so that the dough falls into the pan. Gently tuck the dough into the pan and then peel off the wax paper. Let the overhang drape over the edge of the pie plate, while gently fitting the dough into the pan. Using a knife, cut the excess dough away from the

edge of the pie plate. Use your fingers to crimp the edges of the dough. Refrigerate until ready to use.

To make a partially baked pie crust: Using the tines of a fork, evenly poke holes in the bottom and sides of the crust to prevent it from rising when prebaked. Bake for 8 minutes before adding the filling and finishing the baking.

To make a fully baked pie crust: Using the tines of a fork, evenly poke holes in the bottom and sides of the crust to prevent it from rising when prebaked. Bake until golden brown, 18 to 20 minutes. Cool completely before filling.

To make a double crust: Double the recipe, split the dough into 2 balls, and make a bottom and top crust.

chef's note: To save time, the dough balls can be wrapped in plastic and kept in the refrigerator for 1 week or in the freezer for up to 3 months. Thaw frozen dough in the refrigerator before using.

# vanilla cookie crumb pie crust

## makes 1 (10-inch) springform pan

I prefer using arrowroot cookies by Mi-Del, but if you have a cookie you prefer, give it a try.

1 (8-ounce) bag Mi-Del Arrowroot Cookies
3 tablespoons sugar

5 tablespoons butter, melted
½ teaspoon vanilla extract

Lightly butter a 10-inch springform pan and set it aside.

Using a food processor, blend together the cookies, sugar, butter, and vanilla. Spread the crumbs on the bottom (and sides, if desired) of the pan and press firmly to form a tightly packed crust.

If using the crust with a no-bake filling, bake in a preheated 350°F oven for 8 to 10 minutes, or until firm. Cool completely on a wire rack before filling.

If using the crust with a filling to be baked, fill the unbaked crust and bake according to the recipe directions.

# sugar and oats pie crust

## makes 1 (9-inch) pie crust

I use this crust for my Down East Blueberry Pie. The sugar gives it the perfect amount of sweetness, and the oats give it a hearty flavor. Try it with fresh blackberries or raspberries.

½ cup brown rice flour
½ cup white rice flour
½ cup packed brown sugar
⅓ cup gluten-free oats

⅛ teaspoon ground cinnamon
⅛ teaspoon xanthan gum
⅛ teaspoon salt
8 tablespoons (1 stick) butter, melted

Preheat the oven to 350°F and grease a 9-inch pie plate.

In a medium bowl, whisk together the brown rice flour, white rice flour, brown sugar, oats, cinnamon, xanthan gum, and salt. Add the butter and mix until it forms moist crumbs.

Spread the crumbs evenly over the bottom and sides of the pie plate and press firmly to form a tightly packed crust. Bake for 15 to 20 minutes, until the crust sets and is golden brown. Remove the crust from the oven and cool to room temperature before filling with your favorite pie filling.

# mississippi sweet potato pie

## makes 1 (9-inch) pie

### baking time: 40 to 45 minutes

Oven roasting the sweet potatoes to draw out their natural sugars is the secret to this incredibly delectable pie. Whether served hot from the oven at Thanksgiving dinner or right out of the fridge as a special breakfast item, this "dessert" is a healthful and delicious treat.

2 large sweet potatoes (about 1½ pounds)
1 cup sugar
4 tablespoons (½ stick) butter, melted
2 eggs
1 teaspoon vanilla extract
½ teaspoon ground cinnamon
¼ teaspoon ground ginger

⅛ teaspoon freshly grated nutmeg
¼ teaspoon salt
¾ cup light cream or half-and-half
1 (9-inch) unbaked gluten-free pie crust, such as Buttery Flaky Pie Crust (page 150)

Preheat the oven to 350°F.

Using a fork, poke holes in the sweet potatoes and place on the center of the oven rack. Roast for 1 to 1¼ hours, until the sweet potatoes are cooked through. (Place a baking sheet under the sweet potatoes to catch the drippings.) Remove the potatoes from the oven and allow to cool to room temperature.

Remove the skins from the sweet potatoes and place the flesh in a mixing bowl with the

sugar, butter, eggs, vanilla, cinnamon, ginger, nutmeg, and salt. Using an electric mixer, beat the ingredients together until thoroughly mixed, then add the light cream, mixing until the cream is incorporated.

Pour into the unbaked pie crust and bake for 40 to 45 minutes, until the center is set. Place the pie on a rack and cool completely before cutting and serving.

# down east blueberry pie

## makes 1 (9-inch) pie

Our friend Ellen shared this recipe, as well as the story of her grandmother (Nana) and Nana's dear friend Margarite, who would pick wild blueberries together and then sit on stools on the front porch, gossiping about family and friends. Afterward, they'd go home and make their blueberry goodies. This pie was a favorite dessert served after a big pasta dinner. It was perfected over time, as this summer blueberry ritual lasted well into Nana and Margarite's nineties.
Preheat the oven to 350°F and grease a 9-inch pie plate.

3 tablespoons cornstarch
¾ cup plus ¼ cup water
3 cups plus 1 cup blueberries
¾ cup plus 1 tablespoon sugar

Pinch of salt
1 prebaked Sugar and Oats Pie Crust (page 152)
1 cup heavy whipping cream

In a small bowl, whisk together the cornstarch and ¼ cup of the water; set aside.

In a medium saucepan over medium-high heat, combine 1 cup of the blueberries, ¾ cup of the sugar, the remaining ¾ cup water, and the salt. Cook, stirring occasionally, until the fruit becomes soft and the mixture begins to boil. Add the cornstarch mixture, and whisk constantly for 3 to 4 minutes, until the filling thickens. Remove from the heat and allow to cool for 20 to 30 minutes before stirring in the remaining 3 cups blueberries and pouring into the pie crust.

Refrigerate the pie overnight. In a large bowl, using an electric mixer, beat the heavy cream until soft peaks form. Add the remaining tablespoon of sugar and beat until stiff peaks form. Using a rubber spatula, spread the cream evenly over the pie. Cut into wedges and serve.

# creamy lemon pie

## makes 1 (9-inch) pie

### baking time: 40 to 45 minutes

When we served this on Mother's Day, it quickly became a family favorite. Lighter than a traditional lemon pie, this one is velvety from the sour cream, tart from the lemons, yet sweet from the sugar. It's a dance for the taste buds and a true lemon lover's pie.

1 cup plus 1 tablespoon sugar
4 eggs
¾ cup freshly squeezed lemon juice (from 4 to 5 lemons)
½ cup sour cream

¼ teaspoon grated lemon zest
¼ teaspoon salt
1 unbaked Buttery Flaky Pie Crust (page 150)
1 cup heavy whipping cream

Preheat the oven to 400°F.

In a medium bowl, whisk together 1 cup of the sugar, the eggs, lemon juice, sour cream, lemon zest, and salt until thoroughly blended.

Bake the pie crust for 10 minutes, then pour the lemon filling mixture into the hot crust, lower the oven temperature to 350°F, and bake for 30 to 35 minutes more, or until the middle is set.

Allow the pie to cool and then refrigerate it until chilled. Before serving, in a large bowl using an electric mixer, beat the heavy cream until soft peaks form. Add the remaining tablespoon of sugar and beat until stiff peaks form. Use a rubber spatula to spread the cream evenly over the pie, then cut the pie into wedges and serve.

# aunt lil's creamy cheesecake

### makes 1 (10-inch) pie

## baking time: 40 minutes

America is fascinated with cheesecake. Those on a gluten-free diet can have Aunt Lil's version, a New York–style dessert with a dense filling. The Vanilla Cookie Crumb Pie Crust is superb and takes this rich treat to new heights.

1 (16-ounce) container sour cream
1 cup plus 2 tablespoons sugar
1 tablespoon vanilla extract
4 (8-ounce) packages cream cheese, cubed
4 eggs

1 teaspoon freshly squeezed lemon juice
1 unbaked Vanilla Cookie Crumb Pie Crust
  (page 151)
2 cups sliced strawberries or raspberries

Preheat the oven to 350°F.

In a small bowl, whisk together the sour cream, 2 tablespoons of the sugar, and the vanilla. Set aside.

Using a food processor, blend together the cream cheese, eggs, remaining 1 cup sugar, and the lemon juice until smooth and creamy. Pour into the unbaked crust and bake for 25 minutes. Remove the pie from the oven and gently spread the sour cream mixture on top of the cheesecake. Return the cake to the oven and bake for 15 more minutes. Allow the cheesecake to cool before refrigerating. Top with fresh berries just before serving.

# chocolate and banana bread pudding

## makes 6 to 8 servings

### baking time: 1 hour

This warm and gooey chocolate banana bread pudding is not for the faint of heart. The thick, gluten-free Udi's bagel chunks make for a perfectly chewy and satisfying bread casserole. Serve with ice cream or whipped cream for a special dessert and warm up the leftovers to make an awesome breakfast.

1 (14-ounce) package Udi's Bagels, cubed
1 cup (6 ounces) bittersweet or semisweet
   chocolate chips
1 banana, thinly sliced
2 cups light cream or half-and-half
½ cup packed brown sugar

½ cup granulated sugar
4 eggs, beaten
1 tablespoon vanilla extract
Whipped cream or vanilla ice cream, for
   serving (optional)

Preheat the oven to 350°F and grease an 11 by 7-inch pan.

Place the cubed bagels in the prepared pan, and distribute the chocolate chips and sliced banana evenly on top.

In a large bowl, whisk together the cream, brown sugar, granulated sugar, eggs, and vanilla until smooth. Pour over the top of the casserole and, using a fork, press down on the bread, allowing it to absorb the cream. Let the dish rest for 10 minutes before placing the baking dish in a larger roasting pan. Fill the roasting pan with warm water until it comes halfway up the sides of the baking dish.

Place the roasting pan in the oven and bake for 55 to 60 minutes, until set in the center. Remove from the oven and allow to cool for 15 minutes before serving. Serve with a dollop of whipped cream or vanilla ice cream.

# bittersweet bean brownies

## makes 12

## baking time: 30 to 35 minutes

A new twist and an increasingly popular trend, this recipe makes a nutritious pan of delicious brownies. Black beans replace all the flour, leaving a high-protein, fiber-filled treat will all the classic chocolate flavor intact—a dietician's dream come true!

1 (15-ounce) can black beans, drained and rinsed
¾ cup sugar
3 eggs
3 tablespoons vegetable oil
¼ cup unsweetened cocoa powder

1 teaspoon vanilla extract
1 teaspoon instant coffee granules
½ teaspoon baking powder
⅛ teaspoon salt
½ cup bittersweet chocolate chips
½ cup chopped pecans or walnuts

Preheat the oven to 350°F and grease an 8-inch square baking pan.

Using a food processor, blend together the beans, sugar, eggs, vegetable oil, cocoa, vanilla, coffee, baking powder, and salt until the batter is completely smooth. Using a spatula, fold in the chocolate chips and nuts and pour evenly into the greased pan. Bake for 30 to 35 minutes, until set in the middle and the edges begin to pull away from the sides of the pan. Remove from the oven and allow to cool completely before cutting into bars. The brownies can be stored in an airtight container in the refrigerator for up to 1 week.

# lazy lady's apple crisp

## makes 8 to 10 servings

## baking time: 35 to 40 minutes

This dessert mimics a traditional apple pie, minus the crust. It has tart apples, cinnamon, and nutmeg, and its brown sugar, oats, and butter topping is a "quick fix" for a great pie when you don't have time to make a full crust.

¾ cup packed dark brown sugar
3 tablespoons freshly squeezed lemon juice
1 teaspoon ground cinnamon
1 teaspoon ground nutmeg
1 tablespoon cornstarch
3 pounds tart apples, such as McIntosh or
   Granny Smith
1¼ cups gluten-free oats

¾ cup granulated sugar
¾ cup brown rice flour
1 teaspoon vanilla extract
¼ teaspoon baking soda
¼ teaspoon baking powder
12 tablespoons (1½ sticks) butter, melted
Vanilla ice cream, for serving

Preheat the oven to 375°F and grease a 9 by 13-inch baking dish.

In a large bowl, whisk together the brown sugar, lemon juice, cinnamon, nutmeg, and cornstarch. Peel, core, and thinly slice the apples. Toss the apples in the brown sugar mixture until thoroughly coated and pour evenly into the greased baking dish.

In a medium bowl, stir together the oats, granulated sugar, brown rice flour, vanilla, baking soda, baking powder, and melted butter. Spread evenly on top of the apples and bake until golden brown on top, 35 to 40 minutes. Cool for 10 minutes and serve with vanilla ice cream.

# bard's gold beer brownies

## makes 24

### baking time: 30 to 35 minutes

Adding the rich caramel undertones of Bard's Gold beer to the dark chocolate and molasses gives a new twist to a classic. This is a university favorite!

¾ cup Bard's Gold (gluten-free) beer,
   at room temperature
½ cup molasses
4 eggs
¾ cup sugar
6 tablespoons unsalted butter
8 ounces semisweet chocolate, broken
   into pieces

4 ounces white chocolate, broken into
   pieces
¾ cup Authentic Foods Multi Blend Gluten
   Free Flour
¾ cup unsweetened cocoa powder

Preheat the oven to 375°F and butter an 11 by 7-inch pan.

In a small bowl, whisk together the beer and molasses; set aside.

Using an electric mixer, beat together the eggs and sugar until light and airy. In a small saucepan over medium heat, melt the butter, semisweet chocolate, and white chocolate together, stirring constantly until smooth. Add to the egg mixture and beat until blended.

In a medium bowl, sift together the flour and cocoa; then add to the mixing bowl and continue beating until incorporated. Remove the bowl from the mixer and whisk in the beer and molasses until a smooth batter forms. Pour into the prepared pan and bake for 30 to 35 minutes, or until a toothpick inserted into the center comes out clean. Remove from the oven and allow to cool completely before cutting and serving. The brownies can be stored in an airtight container for up to 1 week.

# butterscotch apple cookies

## makes 5 dozen

Need a break from the same old chocolate chip cookies? Try these butterscotch apple confections made with chickpea flour, cinnamon, brown sugar, and molasses. The butterscotch chips paired with your favorite dried apples make for a tasty new cookie combination, perfect when packing the lunchbox.

1 cup chickpea (garbanzo bean) flour
1 cup sorghum flour
½ cup potato starch
1 teaspoon baking soda
1 teaspoon xanthan gum
¼ teaspoon salt
⅛ teaspoon ground cinnamon

1 cup (2 sticks) butter, softened
1½ cups packed brown sugar
1 tablespoon molasses
2 teaspoons vanilla extract
2 eggs
1½ cups butterscotch chips
1 cup dried apples, diced

In a medium bowl, combine the chickpea flour, sorghum flour, potato starch, baking soda, xanthan gum, salt, and cinnamon.

Using an electric mixer, cream together the butter and brown sugar. Add the molasses, vanilla, and eggs and then gradually beat in the flour mixture until blended. Stir in the butterscotch chips and apples. Refrigerate the batter for at least 2 hours or up to 24 hours.

Preheat the oven to 325°F.

Drop rounded teaspoonfuls of the cookie dough 3 inches apart onto an ungreased baking sheet. Bake for 10 to 12 minutes, until golden brown, allowing the cookies to cool on the pan before removing and serving. The cookies can be stored in an airtight container for up to 1 week.

# bunny's chocolate mayonnaise cake with chocolate frosting

## makes 8 to 10 servings

### baking time: 30 to 35 minutes

Gramma Fitz loves to shower her four grandsons with chocolate treats. For anyone lucky enough to try a bite, this quickly becomes a particular favorite. The addition of mayonnaise makes such a dense and moist batter, which is flavored to the maximum with cocoa, vanilla, and Kahlúa. The extra Kahlúa in the frosting enhances this rich, decadent, and absolutely irresistible dessert.

2 cups Authentic Foods Multi Blend Gluten
   Free Flour
2/3 cup unsweetened cocoa powder
1¼ teaspoons baking soda
¼ teaspoon baking powder
3 eggs

1⅔ cups granulated sugar
1 tablespoon vanilla extract
1 tablespoon Kahlúa liqueur
1 cup mayonnaise
1¼ cups water
Bunny's Chocolate Frosting (recipe follows)

Preheat the oven to 350°F and grease 2 (9-inch) round cake pans.

To make the cake: In a medium bowl, whisk together the flour, cocoa, baking soda, and baking powder. Set aside.

Using an electric mixer and a large bowl, beat together the eggs, granulated sugar, vanilla, and Kahlúa on high speed until smooth and creamy. Add the mayonnaise and beat on low speed until blended. Alternately add the flour and water until completely incorporated. Pour into the greased pans and bake for 30 to 35 minutes, until set in the middle. Cool the cakes on wire racks for 15 minutes, then remove the cakes from the pans and cool completely on the racks.

Using a spatula, spread 1 cup of frosting between the layers and then use the rest of the frosting to frost the top and sides of the cake.

# bunny's chocolate frosting

8 tablespoons (1 stick) butter
⅔ cup unsweetened cocoa powder
1 tablespoon vanilla extract

1 tablespoon Kahlúa liqueur
3 cups confectioners' sugar
⅓ cup milk

In a medium saucepan over medium-low heat, melt the butter. Remove from the heat and stir in the cocoa, vanilla, and Kahlúa.

Alternately stir in the confectioners' sugar and milk until a smooth, creamy frosting forms.

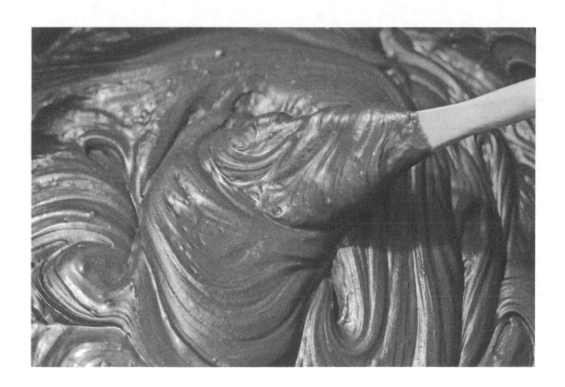

# dump cake

## makes 12 servings

## baking time: 1 hour

Pineapple, cherries, coconut, butter, cake mix, and walnuts—everything but the kitchen sink—and voilà! Out of the oven comes a decadent, sweet, and easy dessert. Serve it warm with a scoop of vanilla ice cream—if you dare!

1 (20-ounce) can crushed pineapple with juice
1 (20-ounce) can cherry pie filling
1 (15-ounce) box gluten-free yellow cake mix

½ cup shredded sweetened coconut
1 cup chopped pecans or walnuts
12 tablespoons butter (1½ sticks), cut into 24 thin slices

Preheat the oven to 350°F and butter a 9 by 13-inch baking dish. Dump the pineapple and cherry pie filling together into the buttered pan and mix together. Sprinkle the cake mix evenly over the fillings, followed by the coconut and nuts. Place the sliced butter evenly on top of the nuts and bake for about 1 hour, until lightly browned on top and bubbly in the middle. Serve warm or at room temperature.

# chocolate-espresso cookies

## makes 4 dozen

## baking time: 1 hour

This recipe comes from friends of the family—specifically from a beautiful and compassionate teenager named Emily, who spends a good deal of time baking and cooking for her father, who follows the gluten-free diet. Her time and talent in the kitchen have already paid off, for these cookies are as sweet as she is.

12 tablespoons (1½ sticks) unsalted butter
1 cup packed light brown sugar
3 cups (18 ounces) semisweet chocolate chips
2 teaspoons vanilla extract
½ teaspoon salt
½ teaspoon baking soda
½ teaspoon instant espresso powder

¼ teaspoon baking powder
⅓ cup light corn syrup
1 tablespoon cider vinegar
2 eggs
3½ cups Pamela's Amazing Wheat-Free
   Bread Mix

In a small saucepan over medium heat, melt the butter and then stir in the brown sugar until the mixture melts and begins to bubble. Pour the mixture into a large bowl and stir in the chocolate chips until they melt. Set the mixture aside and allow to cool for 10 minutes.

Stir in the vanilla, salt, baking soda, espresso powder, baking powder, corn syrup, and cider vinegar. Stir in the eggs, followed by the flour mixture, until thoroughly combined.

Cover the batter with plastic wrap and refrigerate overnight.

Remove the batter from the refrigerator and allow to sit for 30 minutes to warm up slightly. Preheat the oven to 375°F and lightly grease two baking sheets. Drop tablespoonfuls of dough 2 inches apart onto the baking sheets and bake for 12 to 15 minutes, until they begin to look crackly. Remove the pan from the oven and allow the cookies to cool on the pans for 10 minutes before removing and cooling completely on racks. Store in an airtight container for up to 1 week.

# russian teacakes

## makes 4 dozen

The Russian teacake appeared in Russia during the 1700s. The cakes are now commonly eaten at Christmastime, in both Russia and the United States. They are a sweet, dense pastry coated in confectioners' sugar, and they are absolutely Angela's favorite Christmas cookie.

2 cups Bob's Red Mill Gluten Free All Purpose Baking Flour
1 teaspoon xanthan gum
¼ teaspoon salt
1 cup (2 sticks) butter, at room temperature

½ cup confectioners' sugar, sifted, plus 1 cup for dusting
2 teaspoons vanilla extract
2 egg yolks
1 cup walnuts, finely chopped

Preheat the oven to 325°F.

In a medium bowl, sift together the flour, xanthan gum, and salt.

In a large mixing bowl, cream together the butter, ½ cup of the confectioners' sugar, and the vanilla until light and fluffy. Add the egg yolks and beat until incorporated.

Gradually add the flour mixture and mix until blended. Add the walnuts and mix well.

Shape the dough into 1-inch balls and place 2 inches apart on ungreased baking sheets. Flatten the tops slightly using your thumb and bake for 10 to 12 minutes, until the edges are browned. Remove the cookies from the oven, roll in the remaining 1 cup confectioners' sugar while hot, and place on a wire rack to cool. After the cookies have cooled completely, roll them in confectioners' sugar again or using a wire strainer, sprinkle the tops of the cookies. Store in an airtight container for up to 1 week.

# old-fashioned molasses cookies

## makes 4 dozen

## baking time: 1 hour

These tasty and easy cookies are seasoned with ginger, cinnamon, and cloves, but they are nothing like a crunchy gingersnap. Thanks to the molasses, a soft, chewy cookie emerges from the oven and becomes softer after a few days go by. Topped with granulated sugar, these are old-fashioned cookies and probably a favorite of your grandparents.

3 cups Authentic Foods Multi Blend Gluten Free Flour
1½ teaspoons baking soda
1 teaspoon xanthan gum
1 teaspoon ground cinnamon
½ teaspoon ground ginger
¼ teaspoon ground cloves
¼ teaspoon salt

8 tablespoons (1 stick) butter, softened
¼ cup vegetable shortening
½ cup packed light brown sugar
¼ cup granulated sugar, plus more for dipping
½ cup molasses
1 egg

Preheat the oven to 375°F and grease two baking sheets.

In a medium bowl, whisk together the flour, baking soda, xanthan gum, cinnamon, ginger, cloves, and salt.

With an electric mixer, cream together the butter, shortening, brown sugar, and ¼ cup of the granulated sugar. Add the molasses and egg and then slowly beat in the flour mixture until blended. Using a teaspoon, scoop the batter and roll a 1-inch ball with your palms. Flatten each ball, dip in sugar, and place on the baking sheets 2 inches apart. Bake for 8 to 10 minutes, until golden brown, and then allow the cookies to cool on the baking sheets before removing. Store in an airtight container for up to 1 week.

# understanding gluten-free flours, doughs, and batters

## a little of this and a little of that—blending flours

Obviously, for those without celiac disease, using wheat flour is the easiest thing to do, and it works well in all baking endeavors. Unfortunately, for the rest of the world, there is no single flour that can act as a straight stand-in for wheat flour. Blending gluten-free flours is not only a science; it is very nearly an art. When I started experimenting with all the various flours, I often had finished products that were complete duds. Premixed bags of gluten-free all-purpose flour can be quick and easy, but one that works well for chocolate chip cookies might make a terrible pizza crust.

I have yet to come across one gluten-free flour blend that works universally well for all my baking needs. Instead, I have had to learn how to blend my own flours and to make each combination result in the specific flavor and texture I'm looking for in each final product.

There is currently a wide array of gluten-free flours and starches on the market. Some are whole-grain flours such as sorghum, brown rice, amaranth, millet, quinoa, and oat, while others have a starchy carbohydrate base, such as tapioca starch, white rice, potato, and cornstarch. Creating the perfect blend of flours requires mixing the correct proportions of whole-grain flours and starchy carbohydrate refined flours, and sometimes nut or bean flours, like chickpea or almond meal. While there are always exceptions in recipes, due to flavor profiles and textures, the importance of eating whole grains with their valuable vitamins, minerals, and fiber cannot be stressed enough.

When you are feeling adventurous enough to make your own flour blend for baked goods, start with the following method: Combine 2/3 cup of a dense whole-grain flour with 1/3 cup of a lighter, starchier flour. As you gain experience, you will begin to take into consideration the flavor profiles of the flours. Do you like the taste of brown rice flour blended with white rice and potato starch? Or do you prefer sorghum and oat flour mixed with tapioca starch? There are all kinds of combinations, and a little experimenting will help you develop the best blends for your tastes and your favorite foods.

## grinding your own gluten-free flours

Numerous people have told me that they struggle with the texture and grittiness of many of the gluten-free flours sold on the market. This often depends upon the brand of flour you have purchased. I have found that some companies mill or grind their flours finer and then sift them to remove any unwanted debris.

A trick that I use when a flour seems too coarse and gritty is grinding or milling it a second time. I suggest you give that food processor a workout and grind the flour for an extra 20 to 30 seconds and then sift the flour to incorporate air and remove unwanted particles (grit). This will result in a much smoother and less gritty texture.

## on the rise and holding it together—leavening and binding

A leavening agent is used in a dough or batter to lighten or soften the finished product. Several substances will do this. When it comes to leavening gluten-free items, there will be times when just one agent works well and times when several ingredients are necessary. For example, when I make quick breads or muffins, I use baking powder or baking soda along with eggs as leavening agents. It is the perfect combination for getting cakier products to rise in the oven, with the eggs helping by binding the ingredients together. Yeast is the agent of choice for making breads such as Rosemary Garlic Baguettes, Molasses Flax Sandwich Bread, and Grilled Pizza Crust. Yeast not only makes your product rise; it also imparts a uniquely "bready" flavor. You will notice that most bread recipes require sprinkling yeast onto warm water or other liquid mixed with a little sugar. This helps activate or wake up the yeast before you add it to your batter or dough ingredients. In my Sugar-Glazed Cinnamon Rolls recipe, I actually use a yeast-risen dough in which the yeast activation is done in warm apple cider and buttermilk, rather than water, to increase the flavor. If you want your recipe to have more volume and a lighter, airier texture, try beating a couple of egg whites and folding them into the batter just before baking or cooking. This is the key to excellent, fluffy Belgian Waffles.

## layers of flavors—liquids and flavorful additions

One golden rule I routinely stress to students who take my cooking classes is that layers of flavors are key to creating or converting a great recipe. For example, when baking Top-of-the-Morning Muffins, instead of using just milk or water as the liquid, I use applesauce and then incorporate carrots, walnuts, coconut, raisins, and a blend of spices. This enhances the flavor and makes for an unbelievably delicious final product. When making Sugar-Glazed Cinnamon Rolls, I use a combination of buttermilk, apple cider, and walnuts to jazz up the end result. And with my baguettes, I incorporate roasted garlic cloves and fresh rosemary to kick up the flavor a notch. Next time you are creating a gluten-free recipe, consider using apple juice or cider, orange juice, or pomegranate juice; plain or flavored yogurt such as vanilla or strawberry; walnuts, pecans, and pistachios; raisins, apples, blueberries, raspberries, bananas, and cranberries; honey, guava, or molasses as sweeteners; and blends of fresh herbs and spices. These are just a few examples of layering flavors that can bring your gluten-free baking to greater heights. For more information on the most common gluten-free ingredients and substitutions across all areas of gluten-free cooking and baking, please refer to the glossary on page 172.

## staying in shape—types of pans

Baking without gluten has always been a challenge, particularly with gluten-free bread dough, which often turns out more like a batter than a traditional dough. As you attempt to shape it, it can become difficult to handle (a sticky mess), or it may collapse and go flat when placed on a sheet pan. Using xanthan gum or guar gum will give your baked items body and structure, but they still do not have the ability to hold them together in the same way that gluten does. This is one reason many gluten-free breads are baked in bread pans with sides—so the batter can't escape and bakes into the desired shape.

If you do decide to attempt to make loaves of bread without pans, you are going to have to achieve the perfect amount of moisture. If the dough turns out too dry, it will be easy to form and shape on the sheet pan but will bake into a very dry and crumbly product. You will notice in my recipe for Rosemary Garlic Baguettes that the dough is supposed to be slightly tacky and sticky but not overly wet. It is the perfect consistency for forming into a loaf and making a baguette that is crunchy on the outside and chewy on the inside. An example of correct pan choice is in the recipe for Rosemary's Pepperoni-Pesto Cheese Wheels. Again, the dough is sticky and tacky, but it is malleable enough to be rolled out with a rolling pin, filled with ingredients, and rolled up like a jelly roll. The jelly roll form can be cut into slices and the slices placed in large muffin tins. This way, when it bakes, the dough retains its structure and shape. These are just a couple of examples of how pan choice can make the difference between a flop and a real masterpiece.

# the gluten-free pantry

### amaranth flour:
- Made from tiny seeds that are ground into a light brown flour with a nutty and peppery flavor. Can be used as a thickener in gravies and soups or as a flavor enhancer when mixed with other baking flours.
- Store in an airtight container in a cool, dry place for up to 1 month, refrigerate for up to 6 months, or freeze for up to 1 year.

### arrowroot starch:
- A white, powdery, tasteless flour derived from the dried root stalks of a tropical tuber. Can be used as a substitute for cornstarch when cooking or baking.
- Store in an airtight container in a cool, dry place for up to 3 months, refrigerate for up to 1 year, or freeze for up to 2 years.
- Thickening method: Whisk 2 tablespoons arrowroot with 1 cup cold liquid and add to the dish just before serving. Simmer; do not boil.

### bean flours:
**Black bean flour:** Black beans are small beans with a cream-colored flesh and black skin. The flour tends to be grainy in texture and has a strong flavor that can overpower milder flours. Black bean flour can be used in Mexican dips, veggie burgers, soups, stews, and tortillas.
- Store in an airtight container in the refrigerator for up to 6 months or freeze for up to 1 year.

**Chickpea (garbanzo/besan) flour:** Chickpeas, or garbanzo beans, are processed into a very fine flour with a rich, sweet, and nutty flavor. Also called besan flour, it is a staple ingredient in many dishes from India, North Africa, and the Middle East, such as the Indian cheela ka besan, a thin pancake eaten like pita bread. Use to blend with other gluten-free flours and as a binder in bean or veggie burgers.
- Store in an airtight container in the refrigerator for up to 6 months or freeze for up to 1 year.

**Fava bean flour:** Dried favas are skinned and milled into a fine-textured flour with a slightly bitter taste. Because of its assertive taste, this flour should be blended in small amounts with other gluten-free flours in baked goods such as quick breads.
- Store in an airtight container in the refrigerator for up to 6 months or freeze for up to 1 year.

**Split pea flour:** Split pea flours come in yellow or green varieties and have a slightly sweet flavor and a powdery texture. They can be used to make a creamy pea soup or added in small amounts to guacamole, cookies, and muffins.

- Store in an airtight container in the refrigerator for up to 6 months or freeze for up to 1 year.

**Lentils:** Lentils are a staple in Middle Eastern cuisine and are often a substitute for meat. They are used in soups, stews, and salads and can be purchased in flour form and used in flatbreads and baked goods.

- Store in an airtight container in the refrigerator for up to 6 months or freeze for up to 1 year.

**Soy flour:** Made from finely ground roasted soybeans, this flour has a grainy texture and a nutty flavor and is usually combined with other flours for baking or coating. It contains all the amino acids needed to make a complete protein.

- Store in an airtight container in the refrigerator for up to 6 months or freeze for up to 1 year.

**White bean flour:** A mild-flavored flour that adds fiber to baked goods and can be mixed with warm water or stews to make a creamy soup or gravy.

- Store in an airtight container in the refrigerator for up to 6 months or freeze for up to 1 year.
- Thickening method: Beans can be used in the same manner as potatoes or rice. Purée beans together with hot stock and add back into the main ingredients to naturally thicken soup or chowder. If using bean flours, whisk 3 tablespoons bean flour with 1 cup cold liquid before adding to the dish. Bring to a boil and allow to thicken to the desired consistency before serving.

## cornstarch:

- A fine white powder milled from corn and used primarily as a thickener. When blended with other gluten-free flours, it can be used to make baked goods or a crisp coating for meats and vegetables. Its mild taste makes it a perfect vehicle for other ingredients.
- Store indefinitely in an airtight container in a cool, dry place.
- Thickening method: Whisk 2 tablespoons cornstarch with 1 cup cold liquid before adding to the dish. Bring to a boil and allow to thicken to the desired consistency before serving. Boiling too long will diminish the thickening power.

### flaxseed meal:

- Flaxseed meal can be purchased in whole, ground, cracked, or oil form. (The oil is typically served cold on salads as dressings and does not heat well in baking or cooking.) Ground flaxseeds have a velvety soft texture and a slightly nutty flavor. They can be used as a thickener for soups or stews, as a binder for coating proteins such as chicken or fish, and in baked goods such as muffins and breads.
- When adding flaxseed meal to baked goods, it is always a good idea to use small quantities and to blend it with other flours. Flaxseed meal contains a great deal of natural oil that can overpower the flavor of a dish when used in large quantities. Added to pizza crust, golden milled flaxseeds give it a hearty, rich, and nutty flavor.
- Store in an airtight container in the refrigerator for up to 1 year.

### guar gum:

- Comes from the guar plant in Pakistan and is a white powderlike substance used as a binder or food thickener. It is very high in fiber and is used similarly to xanthan gum.
- Store indefinitely in an airtight container in a cool, dry place.

### millet flour:

- Derived from a highly nutritious and versatile grain, this flour is mildly sweet, with a nutty flavor. When blended with other gluten-free flours, it results in lighter baked goods. Try adding millet flour to pancakes, scones, cookies, or quick breads.
- Store in an airtight container in a cool, dry place for up to 1 month, refrigerate for up to 3 months, or freeze for up to 6 months.

### montina all-purpose baking flour blend:

- A commercial blend made of Indian rice grass (not related to rice) blended with white rice flour and tapioca flour. This blend is high in protein, fiber, and flavor.
- Store in an airtight container in a cool, dry place for up to 6 months or refrigerate or freeze for up to 1 year.

### nuts, nut flours, and nut meals:

Nuts and seeds (page 178) have been supplying us with nutrition for thousands of years. Nuts can be purchased either in or out of the shell, whole, halved, sliced, chopped, raw, or roasted. Adding nuts (and seeds) will give your dishes texture, moisture, and, most important, great flavor. Nut flours are ground from the cake or meat of the nut, after the oils are pressed out, whereas nut meals are ground from the whole nuts, making them oilier and coarser. Nut flours and meals add fiber, protein, and flavor to a variety of dishes.

**Almonds /Almond meal or flour:** A nut with a sweet flavor that can be used whole or chopped or ground into a meal or flour. High in fiber and calcium, and rich in antioxidants and phosphorus. Blend almond meal or flour with other gluten-free flours to create nutty-flavored cakes, cookies, muffins, or shortbreads. I like adding a small amount of almond meal or flour to my pastry crusts for an additional rich and nutty flavor.
- Store in an airtight container in the refrigerator for up to 6 months or freeze for up to 1 year.

**Chestnuts /Chestnut flour:** Smooth-shelled sweet nut. Unlike other nuts, chestnuts are very low in fat and very high in complex carbohydrates and protein. They have been called the "grain that grows on trees" and have a mellow flavor. Chestnut flour is used in breads, cakes, and muffins.
- Store in an airtight container in the refrigerator for up to 6 months, or freeze for up to 1 year.

**Hazelnuts /Hazelnut meal:** Also known as the filbert, the hazelnut has a rich and earthy flavor that works well in baked goods, stews, stuffings, and salads. Hazelnuts can also be used to encrust fish, beef, poultry, or lamb. Try toasting hazelnuts to bring out a smoky, subtle sweet flavor. High in fiber, folate, vitamin E, and other antioxidants. Hazelnut meal, made from pure ground hazelnuts, adds a rich flavor to baked goods such as breads, muffins, and cakes.
- Store in an airtight container in the refrigerator for up to 6 months or freeze for up to 1 year.

**Macadamia nuts:** Low in sodium and high in protein, vitamins, minerals, fiber, and antioxidants. Works well encrusted on proteins or incorporated into baked goods.
- Store in an airtight container in the refrigerator for up to 6 months or freeze for up to 1 year.

**Peanuts /Peanut flour:** Peanut flour comes from peanuts that are lightly roasted and ground. "Defatted" means the peanuts have gone through a process to remove their oil. The result is a high-protein, low-fat flour useful for cooking. It should be used blended with other gluten-free flours in baking. Peanut flour can be used in baked goods such as cookies and breads or blended with other gluten-free flours to coat chicken, beef, or pork. Try adding it to chilis or stews to provide a rich, nutty flavor.
- Store in an airtight container in a refrigerator for up to 6 months or freeze for up to 1 year.

**Pecans:** A good source of fiber, vitamin E, thiamine, magnesium, and copper. Pecans can be used to encrust fish, poultry, or lamb, or added to baked goods.
- Store in an airtight container in the refrigerator for up to 6 months or freeze for up to 1 year.

**Pine nuts:** Edible seeds from pine trees that have a soft texture and buttery piney flavor. Pine nuts can be toasted, roasted, eaten whole, or ground into a paste. They are rich in essential amino acids and proteins.
- Store in an airtight container in the refrigerator for up to 1 month or freeze for up to 3 months.

**Pistachios:** The fruit of a small tree native to the Middle East and central Asia, they have a pleasantly mild flavor and can be eaten roasted, salted, or ground up and used to encrust proteins or in baked goods.
- Store in an airtight container in the refrigerator for up to 6 months or freeze for up to 1 year.

**Walnuts /Walnut meal:** Walnuts are very high in omega-3 fatty acids, which assist in lowering cholesterol. They are very versatile, complement both sweet and savory dishes, and can be eaten raw or toasted or ground into a flour and used in baked goods.
- Store in an airtight container in the refrigerator for up to 6 months or freeze for up to 1 year.

## oat flour:
- You can purchase gluten-free oat flour or make your own by processing rolled oats in a food processor or blender. Oats, however, can pose a problem for people with celiac disease, due to issues with cross-contamination. However, a few companies, such as Cream Hill Estates, Bob's Red Mill, and Gluten Free Oats, are dedicated to growing, producing, and packaging noncontaminated oats. These companies produce steel-cut and old-fashioned oats that are certified gluten free. Oat flour adds flavor and texture to baked goods and can be used to bind meat loaf.
- Store in an airtight container in a cool, dry place for up to 3 months, refrigerate for up to 6 months, or freeze for up to 1 year.

## potato flour:
- A light flour milled from cooked, dried potatoes. Used in baked goods, it has a slightly chalky taste and a starchy texture.
- Store indefinitely in an airtight container in a cool, dry place.

## potato starch:

- A flour derived from cooked potatoes that are washed until just the starch remains. Used as a thickener, as well as an ingredient in many baked goods. Potato starch and potato flour are not interchangeable.
- Store indefinitely in an airtight container in a cool, dry place.

## quinoa /quinoa flour (pronounced keen-wa):

- An edible seed from the goosefoot plant, native to South America. It is very high in protein and contains eight essential amino acids. It can be prepared similarly to rice and can be served cold as a salad or hot as a side dish or entrée. When ground, this flour has a slightly nutty flavor. It can be used in baked goods (such as cookies and cakes) to help them retain moisture.
- Store in an airtight container in the refrigerator for up to 6 months or freeze for up to 1 year.

## rice:

**Rice comes in three forms:**
**Short grain:** Has a chewy, soft texture and will stick together when cooked.
**Medium-grain:** It is a moist, tender rice that will cling together when cooked.
**Long-grain:** The rice most commonly used for daily meals. Cooks up light and fluffy and contains less starch than short- or medium-grain rice. Its length is five times longer than its width.

**Commonly used rices:**
**White rice:** Brown rice that has had the bran removed during milling to give us the white polished grain underneath. When the bran is removed, so are the vitamins and minerals. Although brown rice is more nutritious than white rice, from a culinary perspective white rice has a more neutral flavor, which allows it to take on the flavors of other ingredients used in many popular dishes, such as paella, chicken fried rice, and arancini.

**Brown rice:** The whole natural grain, including the bran, which offers protein, iron, calcium, and vitamin B. Brown rice takes 20 to 25 minutes longer to cook than white rice.

**Arborio rice:** A short-grain rice from Italy that is commonly used in risotto dishes.

**Basmati rice:** A long-grain rice from India and Pakistan. Available in brown or white.

**Jasmine rice:** A long-grain rice that has the aroma and flavor of toasted nuts.

**Carolina rice:** A very versatile rice that, despite the name, is grown all over the world. The grains, which are hulled and polished, separate when cooked.

**Converted rice:** This white rice is parboiled to remove its surface starch while leaving many of the vitamins and nutrients intact.

**Wild rice:** Wild rice is not a rice but rather a grass that bears an edible grain. The plants grow in shallow water off lakes and streams.

## seeds:

See Nuts, Nut Flours, and Nut Meals (page 174) for general information.

**poppy seeds:** Poppy seeds are tiny blue-gray seeds that have a nutty aroma and taste. Poppy seeds add flavor and texture to cookies, cakes, and breads, as well as to beef, chicken, pork, fish, and noodle dishes.

- Store in an airtight container in a cool, dry place for up to 3 months, in the refrigerator for up to 6 months, or in the freezer for up to 1 year.

**pumpkin seeds:** Pumpkin seeds are flattish, oval seeds that come from the center of a pumpkin. They are often used in Mexican dishes to assist in thickening sauces. Pumpkin seeds are available in raw and roasted forms. Roasted pumpkin seeds have a wonderful nutty flavor and make a very healthy snack.

- Store in an airtight container in the refrigerator for up to 6 months or freeze for up to 1 year.

**Sesame seeds:** Sesame seeds can be used as whole seeds sprinkled on top of cooked or baked dishes or ground and mixed with other gluten-free flours.

- Store in an airtight container in a cool, dry place for up to 3 months, in the refrigerator for up to 6 months, or in the freezer for up to 1 year.

**Sunflower seeds:** Dried seeds from the sunflower plant that are sold shelled or unshelled, raw or roasted. They can be sprinkled on salads or used in baked goods such as muffins, breads, and cookies.

- Store in an airtight container in the refrigerator for up to 3 months or freeze for up to 6 months.

## sorghum flour:

- A heavy flour ground from a cereal grain, sorghum flour resembles wheat flour and works very well in baked goods such as muffins and breads.
- Store in an airtight container in a cool, dry place for up to 1 month, refrigerate for up to 3 months, or freeze for up to 6 months.

### sweet potato flour:

- A white flour with a sweet flavor and stiff texture, derived from white sweet potatoes. Use in making muffins, breads, biscuits, and cakes.
- Store sweet potato flour in an airtight container in a cool, dark room for up to 6 months.

### sweet rice flour:

- Also known as glutinous rice flour because of its starchy properties, this flour gives baked goods a nice, chewy texture; made from high-starch, short-grain rice. Sweet rice flour and white rice flour are not interchangeable.
- Store in an airtight container in a cool, dry place for up to 1 year.

### tapioca flour:

- Derived from the root of the cassava plant, this flour is very light, powdery, smooth, and tasteless. It can be used as a thickening agent, as well as combined with other gluten-free flours to make delicious baked goods.
- Store indefinitely in an airtight container in a cool, dry place.
- Thickening method: Whisk 3 tablespoons tapioca flour with 1 cup cold liquid before adding to the dish. Bring to a boil and allow to thicken to the desired consistency before serving.

### teff flour:

- Made from small seeds that are ground to a soft and porous flour. It has a faint molasses flavor and may be substituted for other seeds and grains in baked goods.
- Store in an airtight container in a cool, dry place for up to 1 month, refrigerate for up to 3 months, or freeze for up to 6 months.

### white rice flour:

- Made from white rice ground into a powdery, tasteless flour. Usually combined with other gluten-free flours when used in preparing muffins, breads, and other baked goods.
- Store indefinitely in an airtight container in a cool, dry place.
- Thickening method: Whisk 2 tablespoons white rice flour with 1 cup cold liquid before adding to the dish. Bring to a boil and allow to thicken to the desired consistency before serving.

### xanthan gum:

- Xanthan gum is a white powdery flour, produced from the fermentation of corn sugar, that is used as a thickener or binding agent for gluten-free baked goods. It is also used as an emulsifier in many sauces and salad dressings—a must-have in the gluten-free household.
- Store indefinitely in an airtight container in a cool, dry place.

# substitutions

For those who are trying to avoid other allergens, or are just looking for alternative substitutions, here are some suggestions.

## butter

1 tablespoon butter equals

- 1 tablespoon olive oil
- 1 tablespoon vegetable oil
- 1 tablespoon Earth Balance (nondairy buttery spread)
- 1 tablespoon margarine
- 1 tablespoon Smart Balance (nondairy buttery spread)

## yogurt

1 cup yogurt equals

- 1 cup sour cream
- 1 cup coconut or soy yogurt
- 1 cup applesauce
- 1 cup buttermilk

## buttermilk

1 cup buttermilk equals

- 1 cup yogurt
- 1 cup milk plus 1 tablespoon lemon juice or white vinegar
- 1 cup coconut milk plus 1 tablespoon lemon juice or white vinegar
- 1 cup soy milk plus 1 tablespoon lemon juice or white vinegar

## milk

1 cup cow's milk equals

- 1 cup almond milk
- 1 cup soy milk
- 1 cup rice milk
- $2/3$ cup evaporated milk plus $1/3$ cup water
- 1 cup coconut milk
- 1 cup goat's milk
- $1/4$ cup dry milk powder plus 1 cup water

## shortening

1 cup shortening equals

- 1 cup butter
- 1 cup margarine
- 1 cup Earth Balance (nondairy) Shortening
- 1 cup lard

## sugar

1 cup sugar equals

- ¾ cup honey—reduce other liquids in the recipe by 2 tablespoons
- ¾ cup maple syrup—reduce other liquids in the recipe by 3 tablespoons
- ⅔ cup agave nectar
- 1⅓ cups molasses plus ½ teaspoon baking soda—reduce other liquids in the recipe by 5 tablespoons

## eggs*

1 egg equals

- 1 tablespoon flaxseed meal plus 3 tablespoons hot water (allow to rest)
- Ener-G replacer (refer to package directions)
- 1 banana, pureed, plus 1 teaspoon baking powder
- 3 tablespoons applesauce plus 1 teaspoon baking powder

*Note: I have found that eggs are an essential part of gluten-free baking in specific recipes. Here are some suggestions for egg substitutes, but using one will result in a very different finished product.

## xanthan gum

1 teaspoon equals 1 teaspoon guar gum

# techniques for adding flavor

The following techniques will help enhance the flavor and consistency of the crusts, stuffings, coatings, and toppings in your cooking and baking repertoire.

**Toasting Coconut:** Spread shredded coconut in a thin layer on an ungreased baking sheet. Place in a preheated 350°F oven, stirring occasionally for 5 to 10 minutes until golden brown.

**Toasting Sesame Seeds:** In a heavy, dry skillet over medium heat, stir the sesame seeds constantly for 4 to 5 minutes until they become a shade or two darker than normal.

**Toasting Poppy Seeds:** In a dry skillet over medium-high heat, stir the poppy seeds for 2 to 3 minutes, until fragrant.

**Toasting Pine Nuts:** In a small sauté pan over low heat, stir the pine nuts constantly for 5 to 6 minutes, until lightly browned, Alternatively, toast them on a baking sheet in a preheated 350°F oven for 5 to 6 minutes, or until lightly browned.

**Toasting Almonds, Pecans, Walnuts, and Macadamia Nuts:** Spread the nuts evenly in a dry skillet over medium heat. Stir constantly for 5 to 6 minutes, until toasted. Let the nuts cool before chopping or grinding them.

**Toasting Hazelnuts:** Spread chopped hazelnuts evenly in a dry skillet over medium heat. Stir constantly for 4 to 5 minutes, until toasted,. Let the hazelnuts cool before chopping or grinding them.

**Caramelizing Onions:** Place 1 tablespoon of olive oil and 1 tablespoon of butter in a sauté pan over medium-high heat. Add the onion and a pinch of sugar. Cook for 30 to 35 minutes, stirring occasionally, until golden brown.

**Roasting Garlic:** Place peeled garlic cloves in the center of a 12-inch double-layered foil square. Drizzle olive oil over the top and seal tightly. Roast in a preheated 400°F oven for 30 minutes.

**Zesting Citrus Fruit:** Zesting is most commonly done with lemons, limes, oranges, and grapefruits to obtain the outer portion of the fruit's peel or rind. It is used to add color, flavor, and texture to a recipe. Using a vegetable peeler, hand grater, or zester, cut off or grate only the colored part of the peel, avoiding the bitter white pith. If using a vegetable peeler, mince the zest with a chef's knife.

## dusting, encrusting, battered and fried

In *Gluten Free Every Day Cookbook*, I talked about dusting or encrusting as a way of adding flavor to entrées. It's the technique of coating beef, lamb, pork, poultry, or fish with a combination of herbs, spices, nuts, cheeses, and/or flour mixtures (in place of wheat flour or gluten-based bread crumbs) to seal the exterior of a food while enhancing the flavor, texture, and eye appeal of the dish.

Whether you are cooking or baking, the importance of good seasoning, and in some cases even overseasoning, cannot be stressed enough. Dishes served in restaurants often dance on the tongue, simply because they are seasoned throughout the preparation of the dish, not just toward the end. I hope you will enjoy experimenting with dusting and encrusting. Here are just a few ideas.

**Breads:** Place slices of your favorite gluten-free bread in a food processor and blend into a fine crumb mixture. The Italian Herb-Crusted Salmon on page 67 is an example of a scrumptious dish with great flavor and texture prepared with Udi's gluten-free bread.

**Chips:** Using a food processor, blend your favorite potato chips, corn chips, rice chips, or pretzels to a flourlike consistency. This makes for a tasty coating on poultry, pork, or fish. Try the Pretzel–Crusted Tilapia with Dijon Cream Sauce on page 68.

**Coconut:** Use chopped or grated fresh coconut or purchase sweetened or unsweetened grated or shredded dried coconut from your local grocery store.

**Coffee:** Ground coffee mixed with herbs and spices can be a wonderful and unique gluten-free crust for beef, pork, and lamb dishes. For optimal flavor, choose a high-quality freshly, finely ground coffee.

**Cornmeal:** Cornmeal comes in yellow, white, and blue mixtures and is another flavorful option for encrusting proteins such as fish and poultry. For more on cornmeal, see the The Gluten-Free Pantry (page 172).

**Cereals:** Try using gluten-free cereals such as cornflakes and General Mills Rice Chex and Corn Chex. Ground in a food processor to the desired consistency, these make a tasty coating for pork, poultry, and fish entrées. You won't believe that the topping on the Lemon Butter Crumb-Topped Cod on page 69 is made with Rice Chex.

**Flours:** Using different gluten-free flours, you can create tasty coatings and batters that will work on chicken, pork, and fish. Check out the Creamy Chicken Marsala on page 101, the Crispy Fried Calamari on page 122, and the Sesame-Coconut Onion Rings with Orange Marmalade Dipping Sauce on page 31.

**Grating cheeses:** Use hard, dry cheeses such as Parmesan or pecorino Romano mixed with herbs and gluten-free bread crumbs to encrust any fish or poultry dish.

**Herbs and spices:** To build layers of flavor in any beef, pork, fish, or poultry dish, simply blend together your favorite herbs and spices, coat the food with olive oil or Dijon mustard, and roll it in the herb mixture before cooking.

**Instant potato flakes:** Blended with herbs, spices, or cheese, these make an exceptional coating for poultry or fish. Be sure to read the ingredient label, though, as many brands do contain gluten.

**Nut meals:** Nuts are a wonderful addition not only because of the flavor, but because the natural oils will add moisture to the protein as the nuts are adding crunch. The Pistachio-and-Mustard-Encrusted Lamb Chops on page 79 will leave your guests wondering how it could possibly be gluten free.

**Pastry crusts:** When preparing a crust for a chicken or beef pot pie, or for making a buttery, flaky topping for a seafood stew, follow the recipe for my Buttery Flaky Pie Crust on page 150 and the Pie Crust Tutorial that precedes it on page 144.

**Poppy seeds:** Poppy seeds are excellent for coating breads, cakes, cookies, and muffins, as well as for sprinkling over noodles, vegetables, and fish. Toasting poppy seeds (page 182) will help enhance the flavor and give them a crunchier texture. For more on poppy seeds, see The Gluten-Free Pantry (page 172).

**Sesame seeds:** Sesame seeds have a nutty, sweet flavor that works well with many foods. When the seeds are toasted (page 182), they evoke a flavor similar to peanut butter. They can be used to encrust beef, poultry, pork, and fish or added to breads or salad dressings to enhance flavor and texture. You can even use both black and white sesame seeds not only to add superb flavor but also to give the dish visual appeal.

# metric conversions and equivalents

## metric conversion formulas

| to convert | multiply |
|---|---|
| Ounces to grams | Ounces by 28.35 |
| Pounds to kilograms | Pounds by .454 |
| Teaspoons to milliliters | Teaspoons by 4.93 |
| Tablespoons to milliliters | Tablespoons by 14.79 |
| Fluid ounces to milliliters | Fluid ounces by 29.57 |
| Cups to milliliters | Cups by 236.59 |
| Cups to liters | Cups by .236 |
| Pints to liters | Pints by .473 |
| Quarts to liters | Quarts by .946 |
| Gallons to liters | Gallons by 3.785 |
| Inches to centimeters | Inches by 2.54 |

## approximate metric equivalents

### volume

| | |
|---|---|
| ¼ teaspoon | 1 milliliter |
| ½ teaspoon | 2.5 milliliters |
| ¾ teaspoon | 4 milliliters |
| 1 teaspoon | 5 milliliters |
| 1 teaspoon | 6 milliliters |
| 1½ teaspoons | 7.5 milliliters |
| 1¾ teaspoons | 8.5 milliliters |
| 2 teaspoons | 10 milliliters |
| 1 tablespoon (½ fluid ounce) | 15 milliliters |
| 2 tablespoons (1 fluid ounce) | 30 milliliters |
| ¼ cup | 60 milliliters |
| ⅓ cup | 80 milliliters |
| ½ cup (4 fluid ounces) | 120 milliliters |
| ⅔ cup | 160 milliliters |
| ¾ cup | 180 milliliters |
| 1 cup (8 fluid ounces) | 240 milliliters |
| 1¼ cups | 300 milliliters |
| 1½ cups (12 fluid ounces) | 360 milliliters |
| 1⅔ cups | 400 milliliters |
| 2 cups (1 pint) | 460 milliliters |

| | |
|---|---|
| 3 cups | 700 milliliters |
| 4 cups (1 quart) | 0.95 liter |
| 1 quart plus ¼ cup | 1 liter |
| 4 quarts (1 gallon) | 3.8 liters |

## weight

| | |
|---|---|
| ¼ ounce | 7 grams |
| ½ ounce | 14 grams |
| ¾ ounce | 21 grams |
| 1 ounce | 28 grams |
| 1¼ ounces | 35 grams |
| 1½ ounces | 42.5 grams |
| 1⅔ ounces | 45 grams |
| 2 ounces | 57 grams |
| 3 ounces | 85 grams |
| 4 ounces (¼ pound) | 113 grams |
| 5 ounces | 142 grams |
| 6 ounces | 170 grams |
| 7 ounces | 198 grams |
| 8 ounces (½ pound) | 227 grams |
| 16 ounces (1 pound) | 454 grams |
| 35.25 ounces (2.2 pounds) | 1 kilogram |

## length

| | |
|---|---|
| ⅛ inch | 3 millimeters |
| ¼ inch | 6 millimeters |
| ½ inch | 1¼ centimeters |
| 1 inch | 2½ centimeters |
| 2 inches | 5 centimeters |
| 2½ inches | 6 centimeters |
| 4 inches | 10 centimeters |
| 5 inches | 13 centimeters |
| 6 inches | 15¼ centimeters |
| 12 inches (1 foot) | 30 centimeters |

# oven temperatures

To convert Fahrenheit to Celsius, subtract 32 from Fahrenheit, multiply the result by 5, then divide by 9.

| description | fahrenheit | celsius | british gas mark |
| --- | --- | --- | --- |
| Very cool | 200° | 95° | 0 |
| Very cool | 225° | 110° | ¼ |
| Very cool | 250° | 120° | ½ |
| Cool | 275° | 135° | 1 |
| Cool | 300° | 150° | 2 |
| Warm | 325° | 165° | 3 |
| Moderate | 350° | 175° | 4 |
| Moderately hot | 375° | 190° | 5 |
| Fairly hot | 400° | 200° | 6 |
| Hot | 425° | 220° | 7 |
| Very hot | 450° | 230° | 8 |
| Very hot | 475° | 245° | 9 |

# common ingredients and their approximate equivalents

1 cup uncooked white rice = 185 grams

1 cup all-purpose flour = 140 grams

1 stick butter (4 ounces • ½ cup • 8 tablespoons) = 110 grams

1 cup butter (8 ounces • 2 sticks • 16 tablespoons) = 220 grams

1 cup brown sugar, firmly packed = 225 grams

1 cup granulated sugar = 200 grams

Information compiled from a variety of sources, including *Recipes into Type* by Joan Whitman and Dolores Simon (Newton, MA: Biscuit Books, 2000); *The New Food Lover's Companion* by Sharon Tyler Herbst (Hauppauge, NY: Barron's, 1995); and *Rosemary Brown's Big Kitchen Instruction Book* (Kansas City, MO: Andrews McMeel, 1998).

# index

## About the Author

Robert Landolphi is a 1991 graduate of Johnson & Wales University with a Bachelor of Arts degree in Culinary Arts and Food Service Management. He also completed a Certified Culinary Arts Instructor program at Central Connecticut State University. Rob has enjoyed a variety of food-related occupations, including several years as a Wedding Coordinator/Banquet Manager at Glastonbury Hills Country Club, and owner and operator of the Sugar Shack Bakery in Storrs, Connecticut. He currently serves as a Certified Culinary Arts Instructor and Culinary Development Manager with the University of Connecticut. Rob is a member of The National Association of College and University Food Services, the American Culinary Federation, Slow Food International, and the National Restaurant Association. Rob has entertained audiences all over the country with his unique cooking style, personality, and down-to-earth yet informative demonstrations.

Rob's media credits include producing and hosting the *Mangia Radio* show, 91.7 FM-WHUS, and writing and hosting the cooking show *Food for the Journey*. He appeared on Food Network's *How Do You Iron Chef?* promotion program while hosting the University of Connecticut's Annual Culinary Olympics, and on the new cable food program *Boy Meets Still*. Rob was recently asked to appear on CBS's *The Early Show* to demonstrate the intricacies of gluten-free cooking during their "allergy free cooking" week. Local appearances have also been made on *WTNH Connecticut Style News, NBC 30 News,* and the *Better Connecticut* talk show program. He has also been interviewed on numerous "Food Talk" radio programs, including *Everyday Food* on the Martha Stewart Living Satellite Channel, and has shared recipes and industry food trend information with many magazines and newspapers nationally.

Rob is married and has three young sons. He was introduced to the gluten-free lifestyle in the year 2000, when after a lengthy illness his wife was finally diagnosed with celiac disease. Since that time he has made it a personal mission to create and perfect gluten-free recipes that will satisfy even the harshest of critics, including those who do not need to be wheat and gluten free. He is also the author of *Gluten Free Every Day Cookbook*.